The Palgrave Lacan Series

Series Editors
Calum Neill
Edinburgh Napier University
Edinburgh, UK

Derek Hook
Duquesne University
Pittsburgh, USA

Jacques Lacan is one of the most important and influential thinkers of the 20th century. The reach of this influence continues to grow as we settle into the 21st century, the resonance of Lacan's thought arguably only beginning now to be properly felt, both in terms of its application to clinical matters and in its application to a range of human activities and interests. The Palgrave Lacan Series is a book series for the best new writing in the Lacanian field, giving voice to the leading writers of a new generation of Lacanian thought. The series will comprise original monographs and thematic, multi-authored collections. The books in the series will explore aspects of Lacan's theory from new perspectives and with original insights. There will be books focused on particular areas of or issues in clinical work. There will be books focused on applying Lacanian theory to areas and issues beyond the clinic, to matters of society, politics, the arts and culture. Each book, whatever its particular concern, will work to expand our understanding of Lacan's theory and its value in the 21st century.

More information about this series at
https://link.springer.com/bookseries/15116

Daniel Tutt

Psychoanalysis and the Politics of the Family: The Crisis of Initiation

palgrave
macmillan

Daniel Tutt
Philosophy
George Washington University
Washington, D.C, WA, USA

The Palgrave Lacan Series
ISBN 978-3-030-94069-0   ISBN 978-3-030-94070-6   (eBook)
https://doi.org/10.1007/978-3-030-94070-6

Cover illustration: Annika McFarlane/GettyImages.

This Palgrave Macmillan imprint is published by the registered company Springer Nature
Switzerland AG.
The registered company address is: Gewerbestrasse 11, 6330 Cham, Switzerland

The Oedipus complex was the equivalent of what in Physics one calls the problem of the three bodies, a problem for which, as is well known, a complete solution was never found.
(Jacques Lacan)

Care in capitalist society is a commodified, subjugating, and alienated act; but in it is the kernel of non-alienating interdependence and love.
(ME O'Brien)

There is only one misfortune, which is that in our day, there is no longer a trace, absolutely anywhere of initiation.
(Jacques Lacan)

The tyrant who seizes the law is no longer Creon; it is the market that no longer knows any limits, having forgotten the meaning of shame.
(Bernard Stiegler)

For my mother, Eileen

FOREWORD

Homo animal tam familial est quam politicum
Man is an animal that is as familial as it is political

FAMILISM

Tell me how you think about the family, and I will tell you about your politics.

The family has been at the forefront of the Western tradition of social thought; limning the left and the right, liberals and conservatives, the fight against the bourgeois family and the struggle for new family forms, renewed forms of attachment, and postpatriarchal maps of belonging.

Familism, or the centrality of the family form has a long history in social thought. Using it as a Foucauldian *dispositif* or apparatus, let's examine some of the outlines of this construct—insights that can be considered precursors to psychoanalysis.

The family was a kind of microcosm of the state in the Socratic/Platonic tradition. Aristotle attempted to outline a hierarchical model of natural dominance and power based on classical family roles. In the first century CE, Arius Didymus argued that the family is a prototype of the πολιτεία (*politeia* or association, constitution):

> Connected with the house is a pattern of monarchy, of aristocracy and of democracy. The relationship of parents to children is monarchic, of husbands to wives aristocratic, of children to one another democratic.

Thomas Aquinas, who shaped Christian philosophy and ethics since the thirteenth century, updated Aristotle's ζῷον πολιτικόν (*zoon politikon* or political animal), to declare:

> *Homo est animal magis familial quam politicum*
> Man is an animal that is more familial than political.

By the nineteenth century and the birth of the bourgeois family, Marx and notably Engels, concerned themselves with the predicament of the family. This concern with the family forms an early bridge between Marxism and psychoanalysis.

Psychoanalysis is often understood as centering the experience of the family and this is of course accurate, but the way the family takes on significance for Freud is often surprising. Given the medical practice of his times and his own discoveries, Freud usually saw his adult patients alone, on the psychoanalytic couch. And yet there are some notable exceptions: the consultation with a musicologist and student of psychoanalysis, the father of Little Hans, a five-year-old who developed a phobia of horses. He also wrote a famous letter to an American mother concerned about her son's homosexuality, which he described as "a variation of the sexual function" that Freud asserted was "produced by a certain arrest of sexual development." Intriguingly, he was also consulted by the famous Viennese composer Gustav Mahler for his anguish over his lack of progress on his Fifth Symphony in the midst of a marital crisis with his wife, Alma.

During their four-hour walk in the streets of Leyden, the Netherlands, Freud was able to elicit a childhood memory of the young Mahler. Anguished and despondent over yet another of his father's attacks on his mother, the young Mahler ran away from home and in this state, fell under the spell of an organ grinder on the street playing a popular folk tune. Mahler himself connected this with his love of popular tunes, discordant with his serious symphonies. And indeed, following this "walking cure," Mahler completed his symphony, which includes a rather incongruous lighthearted segment that follows the adagietto in the fourth movement. May we surmise that Freud was able to instill in Mahler a similar lightheartedness about his marital woes and allow him to return both to his marital bed and to his symphony? History records that he did (Feder, 2004) Through these cases we have something of the beginnings of child psychoanalysis, psycho-education, and embryonic forms of marital and family therapy. And what they all have in common in Freud's analysis is the

Oedipus complex—in Little Hans, in his psychoanalytic theory of sexual development, and in his understanding of both Gustav's and Alma Mahler's psychosexual history.

Freud also invoked the *family romance* in which children fantasize idealized parents of a higher social class or standing, out of a sense of jealousy (invidious comparison to others) and *parental lacunae*, creating a sort of affective distance. This, in fact, sets the stage for us to understand the development of the Oedipus complex, so key to Freud's insights into child development in the context of what we now call *family dynamics*. In fact, this is the very origin of the term, although it is often invoked without any understanding of its sources in psychoanalytic thought.

The work you are about to engage concerns itself with the plight of the working-class family in our time. The American anthropologist Edward C. Banfield's constructed the notion of "amoral familism" in Southern Italian peasants. He called his study *The Moral Basis of a Backward Society* (1958)—no less! He criticized the peasants for a kind of subsistence morality that mimicked their subsistence rural economy that did not allow for the construction of extended family networks or adherence to other supposed principles of contemporary democracy. As these happen to be my own roots, Banfield's harshly judgmental study was decisive in my rejection of anthropological authority in my university studies. What stayed with me, nonetheless, was the fertility of the notion of *familism*, which is an unacknowledged connecting thread in American social thought.

As the cognitive scientist George Lakoff has argued, the vaunted American "individualism" actually reflects different versions of familism in the left and right. This strikes me as true, with the exception of Ayn Rand's so-called Objectivism, in which she portrayed the individual as well and truly alone with no affective, moral, social, or political attachments to the welfare of others. Rand portrays a world in which the heroic individual is cut free from the bonds of the family. We see this echoed ironically in the dystopian fiction of Yevgeny Zamyatin's *We*, where love and pair-bonding are proscribed; Aldous Huxley's *Brave New World*, where children are born in hatcheries and "mother" becomes a dirty word; and George Orwell's *1984*, where there are no family ties or emotional sentiments. Rand held a circle of the American conservative power elite in thrall for a time but the real apotheosis of this notion was to await the declaration by a woman of real power, Britain's Margaret Thatcher, who famously averred, "There is no such thing as society," demanding that the family and the community could and should assume the responsibilities that the center-left has assured as part of the social contract. Thatcher's vision has not opened avenues of greater personal and familial liberation, but has given way to what Daniel Tutt rightly refers to as a disciplinary and "punitive" social order that affects the contemporary family deeply.

Let me add a borrowed annotation on the very notion of the family. British leftist scholar Raymond Williams has left us a heritage of singular value—*Keywords: A Vocabulary of Culture and Society* (1983). Williams says that the word *family* has an especially significant but difficult social history. Specialists as disparate as anthropologists and sociologists, family studies and family history, and from philology to philosophy have struggled mightily to arrive at a consensual definition, but in fact the protean nature of this biological and social human unit defies all such attempts. And this is the point: just when we think we have captured it, exhausted it, perhaps even tossed it aside, something in, around, and about the family bounces back—through the back door (because we left it to someone else to close the door, the center-right and the conservatives in this case), the basement (due to lack of ontological groundwork), or seeping down from our inadequate roofing (a failure of imagination as much as poor sealing).

Mystification and Ontological Insecurity: R.D. Laing's "Politics of the Family"

Few family therapists or psychiatrists have had the courage to document the tragedies of family life without sappy optimism, bathed in the light of positive psychology and other illusions of our times. Eschewing both mind and behavior, the family therapy movement tried to recast psychopathology in a relational light. Most of its practitioners now rally under the rubric of *systems theory*, referring neither to family relations as such nor to a particular therapeutic approach, but rather to some disembodied principles of systems with the scientific mantle of cybernetics. We can only imagine what Nietzsche might say—*Ecce Machina?*

One exception was the Scottish psychiatrist-psychoanalyst R.D. Laing. Some of his stories were disguised scenes from his own family of origin, as he says in the opening line of his *The Politics of the Family* (1969):

> The first family to interest me was my own. I still know less about it than I know about many other families. This is typical.

"Psychiatry," Laing affirmed, "is concerned with politics, with who makes the law. Who defines the situation? What is in fact the situation. What is in fact the case, and what is not the case. That is, with ontology." Now, this is Sartrean language—the first clue is the word "situation," followed by the core of Sartre's existential philosophy and proposed existential psychoanalysis—"what is the case and what is not the case." Laing has given us such terms as *mystification* (a direct invocation of the Marxian term), *invalidation* (a clinical translation of the core Marxian trope, alienation), and *ontological insecurity* (from the phenomenological tradition) in an approach he called *social phenomenology*. And he brought that tradition to the professions of psychiatry and psychoanalysis as well as to a wider public.

Some 50 years before, German psychiatrist-cum-philosopher Karl Jaspers created a new paradigm for psychiatry with phenomenology, translated by a number of psychiatrists into clinical methods, the most well known of which was Ludwig Binswanger's *Daseinanalyse* or Existential Analysis with his foundational case of Ellen West (Binswanger, 1958). Schooled in mainstream mid-twentieth-century British psychiatry and then psychoanalysis, reading phenomenological philosophy the whole time, R.D. Laing wrote two undisputed classics, *The Divided Self* (1960), followed by *Self and Others* (1961). Before Kenneth Gergen's *The Saturated Self* (1991), before postmodernism and deconstruction, Laing posited the dispersion of self and identity, with its attendant anxieties and insecurities.

Instead of the romantic notion of two becoming one, Laing gives us a vision of the self at odds with and divided against itself, and this opens up vistas for admitting all kinds of psychological and relational experiences on the analytic couch. Furthermore, he attempted to normalize such experiences, going so far as to argue that they were part of a process of psychic exploration and a shamanic journey rather than pathologizing them.

In Laing's model, even the supposedly psychotic experience has meaning if we could only hear it and understand it. It's the same argument as today's evolutionary psychology or neuroscience, but rather than being reductive, it's hermeneutic, leading Sartre to write of Laing and Cooper's (1960) efforts to create "a truly human psychiatry":

Je suis convaincu que vos efforts contribuent à nous rapprocher du temps où la psychiatrie sera, enfin, humaine.

I am convinced that your efforts contribute to bringing us closer to the time when psychiatry will, at last, become a truly *human* psychiatry.

HAVEN IN A HEARTLESS WORLD

In his opening chapter, Tutt writes that

> the family remains a "haven in a heartless world," as the historian and American cultural critic Christopher Lasch put it. How did the family come to exist in this contradictory fashion, placed at the very center of reproducing the bourgeois social order and yet being the only refuge for the proletariat at the same time?

Having been trained by the pioneering generation of family therapists in the 1960s–1970s (see my detailed overviews, Di Nicola 1985a, 1985b, 1997, 2011), I witnessed the period in which Lasch made his prescient observations. As a young therapist, I saw the mental health movement grapple with the sorts of crises that Tutt tracks up to the present. My own contributions to social and cultural psychiatry were triggered by the realization that working-class immigrant families in North America were disqualified as "ethnics" and relegated to a sort of ethnicity museum where we find Little Italies, Greektowns, and Chinatowns, rather than being understood on their own social (class) and cultural (history) terms. Against the American myth of the melting pot, sociologists noted the rise of the "unmeltable ethnics"—mostly working-class groups who decided to negotiate what it is to be American or Canadian on their own terms. My work with immigrants and refugees led to my model of cultural family therapy, using the polysemic metaphor of "a stranger in the family," playing with nuances of alienation and estrangement—the mentally and socially alienated family member as the "identified patient," the immigrant family itself as strangers in a new society, and finally, the alienist (psychiatrist) entering as a stranger in their midst with the paradoxical task of rendering their strangeness more familiar (Di Nicola, 1997).

One of the pioneering groups was the Italian group known as the Milan Team, who tried to place the "identified patient" in her family seen as a system and the family itself in the larger social systems that both shaped and constrained it. Too little is known about Mara Selvini Palazzoli's works on what she called larger systems—hospitals, schools, and community agencies, even to some extent local governments, in such works as *The Hidden Games of Organizations* (1990). The men of the Milan Team—Luigi Boscolo and Gianfranco Cecchin (Boscolo, et al., 1987)—wrote that they were sought out by leftist Italian psychiatrists who were inspired by Franco Basaglia's psychiatric reforms and criticized psychoanalysis as too elitist and too limited. They had a productive dialogue that created a synthesis of social activism with bold new therapeutics.

Along with Belgian Lacanian psychoanalyst Paul Verhaeghe (1999), I am somewhat sanguine about the status of some of Freud's founding concepts, such as penis envy. We think we see it in the clinical material, but those observations are so saturated with social and historical determinants that we can only hazard at what is cause and what is consequence. Here's my challenge: if the family is open to radical redefinition, are not the dynamics of human relationships not also open to a radical revisioning?

So, here's my question: how do we liberate the family not only from this nasty version of what Tutt rightly points to as the symptoms of "late capitalism" (on analogy with advanced disease processes) but from paternalism and patriarchy without losing authority? The French philosopher Alain Badiou has a fascinating take on this problem in his essay on the alienated and transplanted youth of Europe which forms an important backdrop to the crisis of initiation of our time. Tutt connects Badiou's insights to the family in ways similar to those of the Lacanian psychoanalyst Paul Verhaeghe (1999). Verhaeghe asks a critical question which we are only belatedly recognizing but which all child specialists and therapists have seen in their practices for at least two generations: *Where have all the fathers gone?* Verhaeghe situates the problem not with the failure of Oedipus, but with a kind of failure of nerve to assert authority in the West. And he has a pithy quote from Doris Lessing that is apposite:

> It's not that children or youth are more rebellious, more prone to acting out and the rest of it, but rather that we in the Western world are not comfortable with authority anymore!

This appears conservative, but that is a mistake—Lessing was no lesser socialist! We must not abandon the analysis of authority and even power in human relationships to the right and other totalitarian approaches and imagine that we are done with it.

We need to imagine new forms of relating, new ways of bonding, a new kind of "affective commons," using the tools at hand. This is what Tutt's work offers. He grounds the contemporary family in a Laschian critique of the emptiness of modern liberalism, showing how the neoliberal period opens many continuing points of relevance to what Lasch diagnoses in the late 1970s as well as important differences. Tutt opens space for revisioning the family in the light of new social realities and a re-invigo-rated socialism rethought through the prism of Lacanian psychoanalysis.

Against the received wisdom of Western psychology and psychiatry that reason from the individual to the social, my claim is that the family is the crucible of consciousness, the site of subjectivation. Upending the indi-vidualist tradition, I reason from the social to the individual. At the heart of the crisis of the family today is the fact that the family no longer serves as an initiation for subjectivity. Picking up on Lacan's later insights on this point, Tutt connects the decline in subjective initiation with a broader decline in the Oedipal form of subjectivation itself. Congruent with the thought of Bruno Bettelheim, and Gilles Deleuze and Félix Guattari, Tutt argues that initiation is a missing element in our capitalist society which creates a psychic turmoil, and this crisis weakens the family. What would it mean to re-envision the family in this context?

The Family at an Evental Site

In conclusion, we can read Tutt's work as a gloss on Aquinas' maxim:

Homo est animal magis familial quam politicum.
Man is an animal that is more familial than political.

This in turn was a gloss on Aristotle's ζῷον πολιτικόν—*zoon politikon* or political animal—such that Tutt gives a shared voice to the familial and the political:

Homo animal tam familial est quam politicum.
Man is an animal that is as familial as it is political.

As it happens, Daniel Tutt and I share a close reading of the quartet of figures he tasks with revisioning the politics of the family. In doing so, he explicates his wager and stakes, marshalling insights from many disparate sources, including some thinkers who leaned toward the center-right and conservatism later in their thought. The quartet of core thinkers and tradi-tions that Tutt taps into are: Alain Badiou and, behind him, Marx and the communist idea; Jacques Lacan and, behind him, Freud and psychoanaly-sis; the critic of modern liberalism Christopher Lasch and, behind him, Richard Hofstadter and the entire American tradition of cultural history;

and finally, René Girard with his mimetic theory of desire and, behind him, philosophical anthropology.

Tutt's deployment requires an immediate caveat: we are talking about the early Lasch who brought Freud together with critical theory and set his eyes on an interrogation of the American family *before* he became a moralist denounced by feminists and adopted by social conservatives. In the case of Girard, Tutt invokes his quasi-Freudian social theory of desire based on rivalry and competition, rather than his more conservative explorations of the foundations of Catholic thought. What Tutt does, in fact, is to liberate critical thinkers and key ideas from their moorings in their time and even their disciplines to capture a series of *dispositifs* or apparatuses of value in his reading of the contemporary family. He is, in fact, radicalizing Lasch and Girard to make them our contemporaries.

This is a work of both analysis and synthesis. Marshalling arguments, tools of thought, observations, and provocations as *dispositifs* from various sources, Tutt arrives at a synthesis of Freud and Marx, read through new lenses—Lacanian psychoanalysis and Badiouian communism. He lists key concepts, naming them, defining them, illustrating them in a way that the readers can come to their own conclusions, using the volume very much as a kind of conceptual handbook of psychoanalysis-cum-socialism.

This is what makes his project bold and why it demands our attention. While we can debate or nuance his arguments, the project itself is critical and critically important. I would call it a reclamation project—reclaiming the family for psychoanalysis and for the left—and reclaiming psychoanalysis as an investigative tool or *dispositif* for critical theory. Tutt clearly identifies a deficit in works that look at the family from the left and boldly shows that the left needs to learn how to rethink the family. And can we at least agree that most contemporary leftists have nothing to say about it that is fresh or compelling?

Now, in my reading, the most powerful of this quartet is Alain Badiou— "our contemporary Plato" as Slavoj Žižek gushed—and his philosophy of the event (Badiou & Tarby, 2013). By outlining the predicament of the contemporary family, Tutt's text places us at the site of a possible event. As we know from Badiou's theory of the event, even an exhaustive inventory of the elements of an evental site will not allow us to predict an event. An event will not arise from something we already know and possess. It is something new.

What Tutt is offering is nothing less than a clear-eyed inventory of the *evental site* that is the predicament of the family today with a *tour de force* of the arguments and the stakes.

Tutt doesn't know—he can't know—what will emerge, but he pleads the case for the protean possibilities of the family, liberated from its nineteenth-century moorings in bourgeois capitalist society, entering not some imagined future but the full reality of today's society, which is changing under our feet. As Badiou wrote, we are talking not about the delicate musings of "whatever being" in the coming community, the "always already" future of utopian socialism, but the proper human community we live in.

In my reading, Tutt is announcing that the evental site is about to produce an event: a new vision of the politics of the family. We don't know precisely what it will be, what to call it, or what kind of subjects it will produce, much less how to be faithful to its clarifying vision, but we may know the elements in the evental site—the DNA as it were—of what is about to be born: Freudian psychoanalysis, and the Lacanian gloss on Oedipal theory, Girardian initiation, and a renewed socialism, all in the light of the Laschian critique of liberalism. In his sparkling new synthesis of psychoanalysis and socialism, Daniel Tutt is the midwife and the book you are reading is its product. Only you, dear reader, can declare it an event.

Author of *A Stranger in the Family* (1997),   Vincenzo Di Nicola
Letters to a Young Therapist (2011), and
co-author of *Psychiatry in Crisis* (2021)
University of Montreal, Montreal, QC, Canada
November 2021

References

Badiou, A., & Tarby, F. (2013). *Philosophy and the Event* (L. Burchill, Trans.). Polity Press.

Banfield, E. C. (1958). *The Moral Basis of a Backward Society*. The Free Press.

Binswanger, L. (1958). The Case of Ellen West: An anthropological-clinical study (pp. 237–364, W. M. Mendel & J. Lyons, Trans.). In: R. May, E. Angel, & H. F. Ellenberger (Eds.), *Existence: A New Dimension in Psychiatry and Psychology*. Basic Books.

Boscolo, L., Cecchin, G., Hoffman, L., & Penn, P. (1987). *Milan Systemic Therapy: Conversations in Theory and Practice*. New York, NY: Basic Books.

Di Nicola, V. (1997). *A Stranger in the Family: Culture, Families, and Therapy.* Foreword by M. Andolfi, MD. WW Norton & Co.

Di Nicola, V. (2011). In *Letters to a Young Therapist: Relational Practices for the Coming Community.* Foreword by M. Andolfi, MD. Atropos Press.

Di Nicola, V., & Stoyanov, D. (2021). *Psychiatry in Crisis: At the Crossroads of Social Sciences, Humanities, and Neuroscience.* Springer Nature.

Di Nicola, V. F. (1985a). Overview: Family Therapy and Transcultural Psychiatry: An Emerging Synthesis. Part I. The Conceptual Basis. *Transcultural Psychiatric Research Review, 22*(2), 81–113.

Di Nicola, V. F. (1985b). Overview: Family Therapy and Transcultural Psychiatry: An Emerging Synthesis. Part II. Portability and Culture Change. *Transcultural Psychiatric Research Review, 22*(3), 151–180.

Feder, S. (2004). *Gustav Mahler: A Life in Crisis.* New Haven, CT & London, UK: Yale University Press.

Gergen, K. J. (1991). *The Saturated Self: Dilemmas of Identity in Contemporary Life.* Basic Books.

Laing, R. D. (1969). *The Politics of the Family.* Massey Lectures 1968, Eighth Series. CBC Publications.

Laing, R.D. (1960) *The Divided Self: An Existential Study in Sanity and Madness.* London, UK: Tavistock Publications.

Laing, R. D. *Self and Others. Tavistock Publications.*

Laing, R. D., & Cooper, D. G. (1964). *Reason and Violence—A Decade of Sartre's Philosophy, 1950–1960.* With a Foreword by Jean-Paul Sartre. Tavistock Publications.

Selvini Palazzoli, M., et al. (1990). *The Hidden Games of Organizations* (Foreword by P. Watzlawick & A. J. Pomerans, Trans.). Routledge.

Sloterdijk, P. (2016). Fire Your Shrink! In B. Klein (Ed.), *Selected Exaggerations: Conversations and Interviews, 1992–2012,* (pp. 25–32, K. Margolis, Trans.). Polity Press.

Verhaeghe, P. (1999). *Love in a Time of Loneliness: Three Essays on Drive and Desire* (P. Peters & T. Langham, Trans.). Other Press.

Williams, R. (1983). *Keywords: A Vocabulary of Culture and Society* (Revised ed.). Oxford University Press.

PREFACE

This book aims to start a conversation on the politics of the family in our time. It puts forward a theoretical framework for understanding the subjective afflictions that face the contemporary family and points to some ways to think and overcome these challenges. Perhaps unlike other academic works, this book maintains a perspective and a point of view. The author is interested in furthering the emancipatory tradition, that is, the tradition that aims for a more egalitarian and universally just social and political order. The author commits to a class analysis from a Marxist perspective and thus pays particular attention to the working-class family.

This book aims to contribute to the wider debate about the family and offer insights specifically for the left, including the liberal left. It seeks to contribute to three areas of scholarly thought: the first is to Marxist and psychoanalytic debates on the family. Secondly, this book aims to make a theoretical contribution within psychoanalytic theory to analyzing the superego and its status in late capitalism and its role in politics. Thirdly, this book seeks to contribute to a richer theoretical understanding of the legacy of the Freudian and Lacanian theory of Oedipus and how it affects subjective life today.

The introduction is titled "The Family Crisis and Liberation." Here, the politics of the family in the contemporary period are historically situated. The contemporary family is the result of the legacy of the bourgeois family of the nineteenth century and the modern family of social planning developed in the early-to-mid-twentieth century. We contend with the psychoanalytic historian Christopher Lasch, whose work on the American family diagnosed many trends that are still present with the contemporary family.

We then consider the legacy of the '60s and '70s counterculture and argue the "revolution of everyday life" it furthered has mostly been abandoned and resulted in a "hyper-marketization of everyday life" or the tendency for intimate spheres of everyday life, including the family, to be overwhelmed by market and labor demands. This dynamic is not merely endemic to the '60s and '70s counterculture, but that psychoanalytic theory accounts for how any liberation movement may face such defeats in what we call the "paradox of liberation."

Chapter 2, "The Family Spirit and Social Reproduction," begins with a discussion of how the bourgeois family invented a distinct mode of exchange that differentiated the family from other forms of wage labor and how this grants a family with the illusion of their own private existence. Next, we use Pierre Bourdieu's theory of "symbolic exchange" to arrive at a theory for how the "family spirit" emerges within a given family and how it endows the family with a sense of its own uniqueness and separateness from the work of social reproduction.

The family spirit is an invention of the bourgeois family, but the proletariat has always—from the nineteenth century to the present—found a profound sense of subjective value in the bourgeois family, even though it has never been for them. The proletariat only experiences a partial form of the bourgeois family, forced to make it their own. We examine Marx and Engels' critique of the bourgeois family and socialist-feminist critiques of the family, which extend this analysis even further. We analyze the legacy and contemporary role of socialist-feminist critiques of the family and some of the challenges and contradictions abolitionists face today when the "care network" of the family has largely been so thoroughly marketized.

Chapter 3, "The Social Superego and the Paradox of Liberation," analyzes the composition of the social superego, the predominant form of the superego under late capitalism. It looks specifically at the political basis of Freud's discovery of the superego and how Freud's concepts, from Oedipus, to death drive, to the superego, must each be read with an explicitly political context in mind. We then turn to the work of Étienne Balibar and Kojin Karatani and apply their analysis of the Freudian superego to understand the way this concept changes more fully in moments of uprising, political instability, and crisis, and how through this reading we can understand late capitalism as a time that is superego deprived. With this understanding of the superego in mind, we gain better insights into the paradox of liberation and how superegoic dynamics play into politics.

Chapter 4, "The Crisis of Initiation," argues that a crisis of initiation marks our age, and it looks at the concept of initiation more broadly from a psychoanalytic perspective. It then analyzes the Oedipal process and how it was situated in the period in which Freud invented it and how this contrasts with our contemporary age. Chapter 5, "Oedipus: A Function of Initiation," extends these themes by digging more deeply into Lacan's theory of the Name-of-the-Father, his revision of the Freudian Oedipus complex. We discuss the historical periodization of the Oedipus complex and how the Oedipal function works for the subject. We then turn to how a crisis of initiation marks our time and introduce this problem through Lacan's theory of the discourses, specifically the effects of the fifth "capitalist" discourse and its propensity to erode social bonds. We examine how the initiation crisis concerned Lacan in his later years and how it effects subjectivity today.

Chapter 6, "Initiation: René Girard and Alain Badiou," analyzes two preeminent contemporary philosophers and how both theorize the Oedipal drama from a distinctive anti-humanist point of view. However, the two are very different in orientation. Each thinker provides a strategy for resolving the initiation crisis, and we examine the shortcomings and the important insights both thinkers offer to the problem.

Chapter 7, "Accelerate the Social Superego? Critique of Deleuze and Guattari," examines the legacy of the radical and liberatory work of *Anti-Oedipus: Capitalism and Schizophrenia*. This chapter argues the revolutionary anti-Oedipal philosophy and critique of the family developed over this two-decade-long project has not been borne out by developments of late capitalism. Although many of the strategies of praxis developed in this work are valuable—and we discuss them—we argue the project fell sway to the wall of ultra-liberalism, which led to a dampening of the intensity of the project. We conclude with an examination of how Deleuze, in his later work, overcomes some of these political limitations.

Chapter 8, "Liberalism and the Oedipal," picks up from where Chap. 7 left off by looking at how liberal theories of the subject and liberal theories of the promotion of equality and justice perpetuate an Oedipal problem. To drive this argument, we consider two preeminent liberal thinkers: Ralph Waldo Emerson and John Rawls. We locate a similar paternalistic reliance on submission to untranscendable political authority figures in both Rawls and Emerson. We argue this creates conditions that foment resentment, rivalry, and anti-solidarity.

Chapter 9, "The Political Stakes of the Social Superego," discusses the idea of the political and the origin, or "birth," of the political in psycho-analytic theory by considering Freud's theory of the primal father from *Totem and Taboo*. We argue that Freud theorized a distinct "non-subject" at the origin of any emergence of political change and thus of a re-composition of the superego. We then analyze what sort of non-subjects are important figures to think about today. We then turn to a popular culture example of the emergence of the political and a break with the social superego in Todd Philip's 2018 film *Joker* with Joaquin Phoenix.

The conclusion, "Toward a Dialectics of Liberation," considers the superego dynamics on the contemporary left by looking at the interplay between what Mark Fisher called the Leninist superego and the cultural unconscious. The former tendency is militant, ascetic, and tends to be joy-less, whereas the latter is care-based, affective, and tends to conceive of revolutionizing everyday life, thus linking our time to the counterculture of the '60s and '70s.

The conclusion then examines how these two tendencies can introduce a politics of patience to forge greater solidarity and not see one another as antagonistic. Next, we discuss the commune as an alternative form of the family which may help subjectivity more adequately face the crisis of initia-tion and deal with Oedipal dynamics. We end with a discussion of the contemporary working-class family through an analysis of the 2018 *Roseanne* reboot and the revolutionary potential of the black family as two family forms that are essential for any thinking or praxis of family libera-tion today.

Often books that are rich in theoretical concepts make the task of read-ing them more difficult by not defining concepts directly. For this reason, we have decided to provide a Glossary of Key Concepts to help situate the reader more clearly into the arguments.

Washington, DC, USA   Daniel Tutt

ACKNOWLEDGMENTS

This book could not have been written without the support of my wife Beth and my two children Eva and Elijah. In addition, the arguments of this book were discussed and debated and thus made more coherent by the patient engagement of friends and comrades, including Duane Rousselle, Timothy Lavenz, Gabriel Tupinambá, Itai Farhi, Mark Murphy, and the entire community of Study Groups on Psychoanalysis and Politics, a global study collective that emerged at the onset of the worldwide pandemic of 2020. Without this network of philosophers, psychoanalysts, and political activists, I would not have found the voice to write this book.

Praise for *Psychoanalysis and the Politics of the Family: The Crisis of Initiation*

"Freud introduced narcissism late into his science but just in time to witness in light of the shell shock epidemic during World War One the old boundary concept of narcissistic neurosis open wide as a new frontier. Here another norm of adaptation was revealed that plied narcissistic dissociation as the best fit with technologization. Like the French philosophers following the end of the Second Coming of the world war, Christopher Lasch in the United States explored the relationship of the family of Oedipus to the turbulence of narcissistic disorder informing the setting in which psychological and sociological perspectives meet and cross over. Daniel Tutt picks up from Lasch's work, which he robustly revalorizes as prescient, and brings the insights of Lacanian theory and Marxism together to examine the politics of the family today. Tutt shows that the alliance between psychoanalysis and Marxism is truly viable and necessary."

—Laurence A. Rickels, author of *Nazi Psychoanalysis*

"Tutt explores the missed encounter between the radical critique of the nuclear family proposed by the Left in the 1970s and the actual transformations to family structure that accompanied large-scale changes to Western capitalist sociality since then. This book poses serious engagement with psychoanalysts, philosophers, and sociologists, proposing innovative short-circuits between Lasch, Deleuze, Lacan, René Girard, and Alain Badiou. Focusing on the debates around the Oedipus Complex and its social function, the author manages to pave the way for a new strategic view of the family, allowing us to both question the liberal establishment's celebration of the restructuring of family life today as well as to include into Leftist political considerations the relevant aspects of Oedipal subjectivization to social life, aspects which whatever comes to substitute the nuclear family will also have to contend with."

—Gabriel Tupinambá, PhD, author of *The Desire of Psychoanalysis: Exercises in Lacanian Thinking*

"Sociologically, the structure and roles that make up the American institution of the family have changed dramatically over the last few decades. But, unfortunately, the sociological literature has served only to document this change without providing us with a convincing theoretical framework. *The Crisis of Initiation* navigates the structural implications of this change, locating the crisis correctly in the

Lacanian psychoanalytic concept of initiation. Tutt's masterful work demonstrates precisely why Lacanian psychoanalysis and Marxist theory are so essential for navigating our contemporary condition."

—Duane Rousselle, PhD, author of *Jacques Lacan and American Sociology*

"Tutt enters in a critical dialogue not only with Freud and Lacan but also with Christopher Lasch, Pierre Bourdieu, Étienne Balibar, Kojin Karatani, René Girard, Alain Badiou, Gilles Deleuze, Félix Guattari, Ralph Waldo Emerson and John Rawls. The main thesis of the author is that in late capitalism the super-ego is weakened. The author sees two kinds of forces at work: a Leninist super-ego that is militant and a cultural unconscious which is care-based. The author ends by discussing the idea of a commune as an alternative to the family. The book is very enlightening for understanding the changes in contemporary family structures."

—Wilfried Ver Eecke, PhD, Professor of Philosophy at Georgetown University, and author of *Breaking Through Schizophrenia: Hegel and Lacan for Talk Therapy*

"Daniel Tutt masterfully demonstrates that the anti-Oedipal dissolution of the nuclear family was prematurely triumphant. His timely critique urges us to resume thinking about the potential of the family as a site of initiation, resistance and liberation. Essential reading."

—Isabel Millar, author of *Psychoanalysis of Artificial Intelligence*

CONTENTS

CHAPTER 1

Introduction: The Family Crisis and Liberation

Abstract This chapter establishes the importance of psychoanalytic theory for understanding the politics of the family and any politics of liberation more broadly. It begins by situating the politics of the family in the contemporary period, showing how the family is the result of the historical legacy of the bourgeois family of the nineteenth century and the modern family of social planning developed in the early-to-mid-twentieth century. This chapter contends with the psychoanalytic historian Christopher Lasch, whose work on the American family diagnosed many trends that are still present with the contemporary family. It then introduces the psychoanalytic concept of the "paradox of liberation" and discusses the legacy of the '60s and '70s counterculture demands for a "revolution of everyday life" and abolishment of the family.

Keywords Oedipus • Paradox of liberation • Social superego • Cultural unconscious • Christopher Lasch • Neoliberalism

By all measures, the family has undergone a profound transformation in contemporary life, which must be understood from more sweeping changes in the political economy. These changes include the decline of the "breadwinner" family unit, the deterioration of the Fordist wage structure, and its attendant welfare state support, to new expectations of labor

© The Author(s), under exclusive license to Springer Nature
Switzerland AG 2022
D. Tutt, *Psychoanalysis and the Politics of the Family: The Crisis of Initiation*, The Palgrave Lacan Series,
https://doi.org/10.1007/978-3-030-94070-6_1

that require both men and women to engage in labor, typically on a full-time basis, outside of the home. These labor demands have not stopped the increase in demands for reproductive social labor—childcare, housework, voluntary and community work, educational support for children—that fall on the parents and mostly on women. The family has also suffered from the pangs of growing wage stagnation and rising wealth- and familial-based inequality that has taken on a distinct familial source, namely, in the intense concentration of private inheritance. This dynamic has witnessed an increasingly smaller fraction of families to enjoy the benefits of retirement that were more widely available during the Fordist period (the 1940s to late 1970s).[1]

The post-2008 economic crash gave way to a restructuring of the political order, one which governs on a "punitive" basis. As Will Davies has argued (2016), the neoliberal system has entered a stage wherein the primary *enemies* are not external but internal. Its enemies are the working class and the poor. The post-2020 COVID-19 pandemic has opened up a new horizon of this same punitive order that has only intensified the degree of general precarity that weighs down on the family, especially on the working-class family. Many economists have pointed out that family-based inequality remains the primary means for perpetuating a social order so unequal that today's global situation is reminiscent of France prior to its great Revolution (2012).

With these crises bearing down on the family, does the family remain a "haven" in a heartless world, as the historian Christopher Lasch put it nearly 40 years ago? How do we historically periodize the contemporary family? From what crisis is the contemporary family the result? In this book, we pinpoint the crisis of the contemporary family—it's not clear that we can think of the family and crisis as separate from one another today—from the early 1970s with the rise of financial capitalism and a post-industrial economic order that has systematically gutted social protections and fundamentally altered how it dispenses with welfare provisions. This is referred to as the "neoliberal era," and we will use this term to describe this era and our present.

---

[1] To get a sense of how family inequality is at the heart of the capitalist order today, see the argument of Thomas Piketty in his popular work *Capital in the Twenty First Century* (2013). In this work, Piketty argues the failure of liberal and conservative policymakers to tax the estate tax and specifically the inheritance tax of families is a major, if not *the* major, driver of wealth inequality.

We are not only interested in understanding the family as a unit of political economy. Instead, we aim to arrive at a theory that can tie together the peculiar intersection of the family, where the economic, the cultural, the personal, the social, the political, and the individual all meet. The family is, after all, assigned the task of socializing children in a delicate balance of discipline, education, instruction, and preparation for entering the labor market. Psychoanalysis offers the best theory to account for how all these nodes of socialization meet up and interact. It shows how the family functions as a site overloaded with identifications and affects directed at (and by) parents, or surrogate parents, and the myriad of ways these identifications and affects are managed, contested, and worked through in the broader process of socialization and subjectivity.

What psychoanalysis offers to the politics of the family is a theory of how subjects—both parents and children—process various forms of psychic ambivalence and guilt that stem from familial identifications in regions of the unconscious. This theory is the infamous "Oedipus complex" coined by Freud to refer to a theory of how the subject, or self, overcomes the aggressive primary stages of narcissism through identification with the parents and how this working-through of identifications and affects is key to psychic autonomy and liberation. Lacanian psychoanalysis offers both a different account of this drama of identification and working-through, and an updated historical account of Oedipus, proposing that a crisis of Oedipus marks our contemporary culture.

Today, the family is tasked with overseeing a socialization process wherein the Oedipal dynamics no longer adequately describe the scene and drama of subjectivity that Freud theorized. According to many psychoanalysts, our age is marked not by a decline in the Oedipus function but by a crisis of Oedipus, which has led many thinkers to ask whether our culture is "post-Oedipal."[2]

We call for a re-appraisal of Oedipus, knowing full well that the Oedipal myth is multifaceted and that its function is a matter of debate and

---

[2] The argument that late capitalist society is "post-Oedipal" has two variances; the first is clinical. Several psychoanalysts point to clinical cases and examples that show post-Oedipal symptoms in analysands are more common; see Sanja Borovečki-Jakovljev and Stanislav Matačić, "The Oedipus Complex in Contemporary Psychoanalysis" Coll. Anthropology 29 (2005) 1: 351–360. The other theory of the rise of the "post-Oedipal" is a theory derived from psychoanalytic social theory. We see this argument emerge in several Lacanian theorists, which is an insight initiated by Lacan's later work of de-mythologizing the Oedipus complex. This book tracks these insights and remains in dialogue with this literature very closely.

dispute. There is a strange death-driven immortality to Oedipus, which is revealed in the last part of Sophocles' play "Oedipus at Colonus," where Oedipus roams the desert, blinded to his fate but lost to the world. Oedipus only lives on as a specter, a blind function *we thought we had killed* but somehow remains among us all the same. Oedipus is hard to kill, and rumors of his untimely demise have been greatly exaggerated.

Ever since the rise of the modern bourgeois family structure in the early nineteenth century on through its dissolution in the late nineteenth century, and into the rise of the family of social planning steered by bureaucratic oversight in the 1920s onward, the family has been presented as "separate" from society. But this separateness is nothing but an illusion that relies on an ideology to maintain. Simultaneous to the family's supposed private existence, the family is placed at the locus of social reproduction; it is designed, crafted, and structured by forces of production and class hierarchy. But despite this important contradiction of the family—a problem we address in Chap. 2—the family remains a "haven in a heartless world," as the historian and American cultural critic Christopher Lasch put it. But how did the family come to exist in this contradictory fashion, placed at the very center of reproducing the bourgeois social order and yet being *the only refuge* for the working class at the same time? To answer this question, we begin with a historical periodization of the family from the lens of Marxist and social reproduction theory.

To understand the politics of the family, we must situate the contemporary family from its bourgeois origins in the post-French Revolutionary world up to the present and expand on this peculiar *neutral* or *separate* status of the family. How does the family come to be seen by its members and as a wider institution in society as separate from social reproduction? This illusion of the family's separateness relies on a sophisticated ideological mechanism. It can often feel a shock to learn that the family is an invention designed by social scientists and shaped by forces of capitalist production and class to further a system of reproductive social labor. There is something too much of the real, something too perhaps alienating in that realization especially given the family is a site of intimate care and affection. The family in our time is meant to serve as a receptacle for the fallout and the failures of society; it is intended, especially in the neoliberal era, to make up for the loss of the welfare state and other social protections.

In the early twentieth century, the model and design of the family was a creation of social scientists: behaviorists, psychologists, psychoanalysts, and sociologists. They furthered a version of the family that was to be tasked with social reproduction and meant to be separate from society yet united by the "interpersonal relations of its members" (Lasch, 1976, p. 43). In this vision, the family was meant to serve as a *neutral site* where emotional person-making and development can occur, that is, where the emotions otherwise inappropriate to express in the workplace can find an outlet. Thus, the family was conceived as a training ground and relay system to the social field. It was this relay system of the family which was called upon to cultivate the child's introduction to the social: the workplace, the school, and institutional life. This version of the family was reliant on a successful Oedipal process.

By Oedipal process we refer to the working-through of identifications, attachments, and affects that are bound up with the child's relations to the parents and the family and importantly bound up with forces extending far beyond the family. What the neoliberal era opens is a profound fragmentation to this very process. The family is now far more precarious, and this model of the family has broken apart at the seams. Its one-time private separateness is now thoroughly socialized.

In many ways, Christopher Lasch is the interlocutor we must wrestle with to situate the psychoanalytic politics of the family today. Lasch's widely read 1979 book *The Culture of Narcissism: American Life in an Age of Diminishing Expectations* remains an important reference point for the contemporary left.[3] This work has produced a series of debates among the contemporary socialist, populist, and liberal left over the question of the nostalgia for the family of the mid-twentieth century post-war welfare state. Lasch's politics have been assessed as everything from socialist to populist to neoconservative and his thought is often associated with moralism and traditionalism. In this work we are less interested in his moral-political insights as much as we are in furthering and critiquing his

---

[3] In the post-2016 period, Christopher Lasch's thought has experienced a resurgence in popularity among both new socialists and more tradition-oriented left liberals. These audiences tend to read Lasch as an anti-elitist populist social democrat. This community also finds Lasch's critique of the liberal intelligentsia: feminists, radical Marxists, and so on as a source for critiquing the contradictions on today's left, from corporate feminism to hypocritical tendencies among radical leftists and their complicity with the liberal order. This community is often referred to as the "post-left" in social media parlance. We hope that the critique we offer of Lasch's theories might contribute to adding more perspective to this resurgence of interest in Lasch.

theoretical insights, which remain deeply insightful for any understanding of the politics of the family.

We will argue that while Lasch's nostalgia for the early welfare state and later turn to social conservativism and even neoconservative politics is problematic for any left-oriented position, his analysis of the crisis of the family and the broader cultural crisis of American—and by now global—society presents several concepts from psychoanalytic theory that are worth retaining. While Lasch's theories are essential, we will break with him on theoretical grounds with his theory of ideals and identification.[4] Lasch frames the historical shift to the new arrangement of the family as concurrent with a wider trend among the cultural intelligentsia: writers, artists, and activists who faced this tumultuous period of the transition from the 60's cultural revolution to the triumph of finance capitalism and neoliberalism as a liberatory opportunity for self-expression and individual liberty.

The contemporary family is split in its composition. It is founded on a disciplinary class system tasked with reproducing an unjust social order and simultaneously possessing the trappings of collective demands of liberation and freedom. Many feminist writers commenting on the rise of the neoliberal era were writing when the social order was experiencing a decline in patriarchy and a general opening of subjective freedom. We track this complex split between the decline of patriarchal authority and the supposed decline of Oedipus as concurrent with this new, hyper-socialized family thrown into the cycles of capitalist accumulation. That this new organization of the family was seen by many as a liberatory design of the family remains a contradiction that plagues our cultural unconscious.[5]

---

[4] While we are critical of Lasch at points, we are interested in offering a corrective to some of his more contemporary critics: Lasch is not a left populist solely interested in a revanchist anti-elitism, but much of his earlier work grounds a psychoanalytic analysis in a Marxist analysis of culture and society. At later points we consider Lasch's critics, specifically the most thoughtful feminist writers that offered critiques of his work, especially the idea that Lasch insists on a society in which the father's authority is affirmed and centered.

[5] The contradictions of the cultural revolution of the 60's and 70's revolve in many ways around the political contestation over the family and this contestation has been reacted to by the right in the turn to "family values" in the early 1980s with the rise of neoliberalism. This terrain of political contestation involves, psychoanalytically speaking, a confrontation with what Ellen Willis calls the "cultural unconscious" and it has, importantly, been a terrain that the right tends to monopolize. Any leftwing movement must reconcile these contradictions and speak to the politics of the cultural unconscious. If the left wants to take seriously the

It is difficult to derive a theory of the contemporary family that considers all the myriad ways in which the lived experience of the family takes shape, given how much the family seems to exist in a state of permanent crisis, from the 2008 economic crash to the 2020 COVID-19 health pandemic. Therefore, the family today is thought of, to deploy a term that is prized by neoliberal ideologues, as a "resilient" form (Leary, 2018).[6] One striking fact about the family in contemporary political and social discourse is that the fantasy of a "more stable family" permeates the broader political conversation in often direct and unconscious ways. The fantasy of the Fordist family structure with the "Breadwinner" father was a short-lived, post-World War II social promise that was always racially exclusive in its promise, and it quickly fizzled out by the mid-to-late 1970s. Yet, the cultural unconscious today is still driven by this fantasy of lost family stability and this fantasy animates political controversies and debates.

The stable family fantasy is itself a contradiction that is rooted in a nostalgia for a more properly privatized bourgeois family where greater leisure time and family agency was available. Much like Lasch's longing for a return to early New Deal welfare state social life, our contemporary politics is animated by a similar nostalgia for a return to an imagined welfare state panacea, a vague Golden Age. This Golden Age is not only celebrated by conservatives or "pro-family values" Christians, or by "Make America Great Again" slogans. What animates these slogans are demands for a family of leisure and adequate free time, where experimentation in self-making is both present and possible, as opposed to the family of neoliberalism that is filled with constant labor, activity, and toil. Our cultural unconscious conceals within it a desperate and unconscious yearning, a utopia even. It is this longing that animates our cultural unconscious. This longing is shrouded in an ambivalence over the past, expressed in the contemporary culture wars that trade off in imaginary contestations over this collective

---

cultural unconscious at stake in politics, it needs to learn to talk differently about the politics of the family and the insights of psychoanalysis can be of assistance in this regard.

[6] John Leary defines the use of "resilience" in our time in the following way: "The quality or fact of being able to recover quickly or easily from, or resist being affected by, a misfortune, shock, illness, etc.; robustness; adaptability." "Resilience" is everywhere, its popularity rising proportionally with the dangers, or perceptions of dangers, facing the planet: climate change, food shortages, financial crisis, or for the Wall Street journal crowd, strikes (also fire and hurricanes). See Leary (2015), *Keywords for the Age of Austerity 19: Resilience* from Leary, J. (2018) *Keywords: The New Language of Capitalism* (2018) Chicago: Haymarket Books.

longing. But one thing is for sure in these debates: the family's illusion as a private and sealed-off indifferent or neutral space has completely eroded. This erosion accelerates a politics of nihilism, resentment, and political impotence.

The family in the neoliberal era is more constrained and more thrown into the levers, gears, and mechanisms of the social reproductive process than the family has ever been before, and this has led to an intensification of family precarity and family fragility. This fragility affects the politics of the family because it limits the possibilities of experimentation with envisioning or enacting political transformation of the family, and by extension political transformations more broadly. Quite simply, working-class people don't have the leisure time to experiment in communal family forms that were prominent in the 1960s and 1970s counterculture, nor do working-class people experience the fantasy of the stable Breadwinner family unit. In mainstream debates over the family, feminism, abortion and related topics, this politics of nostalgia for a return to the Breadwinner family itself often leads critics to call defenses of the family implicitly anti-feminist or pro-patriarchy.

The intensifying family precarity in today's time has not prevented socialist-feminists from proposing family abolition, and there is a resurgence of calls for family abolition. These demands must contend with the precarity constraints that face the contemporary family and the added dynamic that the family remains a "haven in a heartless world," even—and possibly especially—for the working class. Ideologically speaking, the task of the family today is to succeed, at all costs, in reproducing subjects capable of realizing and maximizing their destiny on the market. The Oedipal process thus remains at the heart of the contemporary family in the sense that it is a pragmatic part of the reproductive process itself, that is, working-through affective attachments to parents is an important part of entering the workforce, the corporation, the school, and so on even though this process has been strained and stunted in our time. The family is tasked, far more than the historical bourgeois family ever was, with managing children's affective, financial, educational, and moral instruction and they receive a whole set of impersonal apps and social instrumentations to assist in this labor.[7]

---

[7] Melinda Cooper's *Family Values: Between Neoliberalism and the New Social Conservatism*, Zone Books, 2017 offers t-->"?>he best analysis of the changing dynamics of the neoliberal family. We utilize and turn to Cooper's insights throughout this work. One of the most

In *The Culture of Narcissism,* Lasch (1991) identifies a series of paradoxes: just as American culture witnesses a massive turn to a focus on inward life, the very core of inner life can no longer be taken seriously by the leading writers and artists. A profound hollowness permeates the creative classes. No longer do fathers, preachers, and teachers initiate their pupils, children, or students into new stages of maturity or development, but a different, more seemingly "social" superego replaces these ego ideals. Lasch waged a Jeremiad against the cultural and political changes that brought the social superego about, insisting that this opening of the social superego was not a liberatory moment but a process that was producing profound emptiness and aggressiveness. The social superego, for Lasch, signaled a decline in the effective function of the Oedipus complex and he argued it brought about the "culture of narcissism." This shift is historically accounted for in the very subtitle of his book: the *age of diminishing expectations.*

Just as there is a decline in Oedipus, there is a twofold diminishment: both in what we can expect from the future and a fragmentation in the structure of the bourgeois family and its former stability. As these social and cultural changes were accelerating, the liberal and progressive left, along with the literary and cultural commentariat, tended to embrace these transformations as *forms of liberation,* often welcoming the changes as offering more room for horizontal organization of work and family life, freer self-expression, and a loosening of patriarchal authority. But the liberty implicit in these changes was only partially capable of being realized because they were reliant on the accelerating marketization of everyday life. That is, the problem resided in the fact that these liberation mechanisms were all discoverable only via the market, not via a continued and patient political experimentation in the family form itself. There is thus an unmet and ongoing series of demands that we have inherited from this period of liberation that is worth re-opening, re-investigating and creatively experimenting with.

important insights of Cooper's work is the political insight that the construction of the neoliberal family is not to be understood as a liberal or conservative invention, but an invention and process that has combined both liberal and conservative policymakers, the function of the family is not really in dispute among the democratic and parliamentary order in any meaningful way. Therefore, in part, we insist that any thinking of a liberation for and of the family today must tether with the emancipatory tradition, socialist-feminism, and other abolition traditions of thought. The current political order cannot assist a liberatory project for the family -->"?>today.

What does a liberated family look like? How do the arrangements of labor, of hierarchy, childrearing, and divisions of labor function within a family when they are not tethered to the bourgeois family form and its private existence? Part of the reason the liberationist demands of the cultural revolution of the '60s and '70s failed is because it gave up on the patience needed to continue experimenting with alternatives to the family form. As a result, the demands of radical socialist-feminists and the left were generally only partially met because their realization was satisfied in the market sphere. These political and cultural changes mark the neoliberal era, and these changes also witness the intensification of bureaucracy and experts over the domains of personal relations (intimate life, friendship, and the family), the rise of a culture dominated by images, the expansion of consumerist techniques of social life, and new therapeutic and self-help ideologies.

This argument has some precedents, and a similar analysis is made in Luc Boltanski and Eva Chiapello's *The New Spirit of Capitalism* (1999). They argue the liberationist demands of the 1968 protest movements—and the wider spirit of the '60s and '70s—that advocated free expression, horizontal social relations, and more general cultural-libertarian demands led to co-optation of these demands in the market sphere. Most notably, this co-optation was evident in the fact that much of the business and corporate management literature adopted the slogans, mantras, and worldview of the protest ideology and integrated much of it within workplace cultures. Thus, Lasch, Chiapello, and Boltanski help us identify a deeper psychoanalytic insight, what we will call the "paradox of liberation."

This paradox functions in the following way: *liberationist social change leads to a decline in ego ideals and, by extension, a change in the composition of the superego.* This paradox is already opened in Freud's ground-breaking work *Beyond the Pleasure Principle*, published in 1920 following the collapse of the withering aristocratic Austro-Hungarian Empire. It is important that this political context in which Freud's text was written be noted as it involved the collapse of the aristocracy and all the attendant collapse of the psychic order it afforded. It was also a profound liberationist moment across Europe as the Russian Bolshevik revolution encircled Europe, posing the possibility of a mimetic contagion of emancipation to other European countries, most notably Germany and France. We will show that Freud fused these two political forces, and the insight of the superego, as we will develop in Chap. 3, is attentive to the paradox of liberation. At the heart of the paradox of liberation is Freud's entirely novel theoretical account of the death drive as an internal source of aggressive repetition compulsions.

In Chap. 3, we discuss the political dynamics that underpin Freud's discovery of the superego and the death drive. We examine what the superego is and how it functions politically. We pinpoint two superego dynamics: superego as a regulator of conscience and psychic censorship, and later, after Freud invents the death drive, the superego is mediated by the death drive and the forms of inner aggression it takes on.[8] The paradox of liberation is a concept that informs a logic of historical change as well as sheds insight for movements of social and political emancipation, revealing the double-edged basis of social liberation and the psychic structures that regulate that change and ultimately work to moderate it. The paradox of liberation invites us to distinguish *between liberation and emancipation as two different logics and axioms of social and political change.* This paradox is a gift of psychoanalytic thought to emancipatory politics, an instruction in how certain impediments to universal change arise in historical situations of revolution and transformation.

Although Lasch (1991) is primarily focused on the transformations taking place in the late 1970s, he does provide a historical genealogy of narcissism as a structure of social life across three distinct historical periods. The first period coincides with the well-theorized idea of the influence of the Protestant Work Ethic that runs through American culture since its founding up to the second World War.[9] In this stage, social recognition was determined based on one's individual relation to God and work, an

---

[8] This contrast between inner aggression of the death drive and the superego theorized as an external censor is at the heart of the paradox of liberation: namely, it points to the way in which events of political and social liberation or emancipation modify this very point of contrast. We examine the extent to which this shift in superego and the rise of the social superego is not merely a phenomenon of our neoliberal era. It is also present in historical periods in which liberatory events produce such effects on the family and institutional and cultural life more generally.

[9] The Protestant subconscious is an important motif in sociological and historical accounts of American civic and social life. Lasch locates the decline in the efficacy of this Protestant subconscious in the period immediately following the New Deal where a more egalitarian conception of government was temporarily triumphant. To learn more about the hugely influential work on the theory of the Protestant work ethic, see Weber, Max. (2002) *The Protestant Ethic and the Spirit of Capitalism: And Other Writings.* 1st ed. New York: Penguin Books.

individualized relation of self-recognition, and it was marked by a histori-cal connection to family, community, and tradition (Weber, 2002).

The second stage of narcissism Lasch identifies as the "heteronomous man of organization" whereby recognition from others was realized through institutions. This period reached a zenith in the post-New Deal period. In this period, narcissism was largely held in check through social relations that enabled "socially determined ego identification" with others (Lasch, 1991, p. 7). The subject, or tendency of self-making in this second stage, perceives the game's rules (competition, advancing in one's work-place, etc.) in terms of the ideal Ego grounded in social relations. It is this early Fordist stage that presented a type of Eden or panacea for Lasch. It is thus not exactly the broader "welfare state" that produces a nostalgia for a specific period in American life. Thus, to the extent that we can critique Lasch as a nostalgic thinker, it is more productive to locate the period for which Lasch is nostalgic in the short-lived, immediate post-New Deal period and the institutional and comradery this period afforded.

In any event, it is these prior two stages that kept narcissism in check, whereas the third stage, which can be read as the disintegration of the post-New Deal welfare state began with the onset of early financialization of the economy in the 1970s. This period has only accelerated and intensi-fied narcissism. From the early 1970s to the present Lasch argues narcis-sism becomes more prone to pathological and fundamentally aggressive tendencies. But these tendencies of narcissism are not meant to be con-strued as particularly extreme. To the contrary, it is the pervasively moder-ate yet ubiquitous normalization of these forms of narcissism that Lasch so carefully picks up on. The normalization of pathological narcissism devel-ops when the ego cannot differentiate itself from objects around it and it is this phenomenon that marks the culture of narcissism.

Thus, the culture of narcissism is one in which the ego ideals that used to provide a reprieve to secondary narcissism have grown defective or inoperative. In the space of this in-operativity of ideals emerges the "social superego" as a functional stand-in authority. The social superego is found in the common observation of therapists, both psychoanalytic and beyond, that patients tend to "act out their problems, they do not repress them." This shift in the superego leads to a growing sense of inner aggression. Still, this inner aggression is also routed effectively into market logics of career advancement, which led to a culture that normalizes megalomania-cal pursuit of success and an increasing difficulty in forming positive iden-tifications with other people's achievements.

Lasch's analysis of the collapse of ego ideals and the rise of a pernicious type of social superego (1991) provides an incredibly useful way of situating psychic subjectivity in the broader period of neoliberalism and its attendant marketization of everyday life. But what about the effects of these changes at the social and economic policy level? Melinda Cooper (2017) points out in her important work, *Family Values: Between Neoliberalism and the New Social Conservatism*, that in the neoliberal turn to dismantle the Fordist welfare state in the 1970s, there was an explicit political strategy to make the family serve as the "elementary form of private wealth accumulation" (Cooper, 2017, p. 16). To achieve this, both the social conservative and liberal wings of policymakers, politicians, and business leaders formed a consensus around the preservation of the family as the *primary bulwark* to lean on in the absence of a stable welfare state. This insight reveals the properly "political" dimension to the wider economic changes brought about by financialization and a turn to a growing post-industrial economy.

The premise of the bourgeois family, namely, that it be "separate" from the demands of the market completely breaks down. Moreover, this new structure and design of the family is one in which the family must take on the massive responsibilities that come in the wake of the state no longer providing welfare protections: the family is over-worked, exhausted, and rendered more fragile all the while heavily disciplined to social market logics. This process both is profoundly precaritizing and massively increases the responsibility placed on the family.

The politics of the family has been at the very center of political debate and contention during the neoliberal era, from the Christian right and "family values" in the United States to leftist demands for the abolition of the family. The spectrum of political contestation over the family revolves around this highly marketized and radically socialized version of the family, and it remains a terrain of the "cultural unconscious" (Willis, 2014). The cultural unconscious refers to the libidinal stakes of the family and its role in the social order. It refers to the desires and unfulfilled demands for enjoyment and leisure the family promises. It is the contestation over the cultural unconscious that reveals the family as a social phenomenon, from the socialist-feminist plea for the abolition of the family to liberal and conservative calls to make the family more flexible and adaptable to capitalist life to conservative family values movements; the cultural unconscious is the psycho-political terrain in which these politics occur.

The discourse on the politics of the family becomes marked by the sense that each side swaps in mutual caricatures of the others argument: the left sees only a return to tradition and patriarchy, the right sees radical family abolitionism even in neoliberal centrist reformists who desire nothing close to such demands. This creates a certain hysteria of the cultural unconscious, which—as Ellen Willis shows—the right tends to speak to more coherently than the left. After all, from a libidinal point of view, the right tends to name the crisis of the marketization of the family head-on and either in attacking the left as outrageous in its calls for family abolition or by its own demands for a return to traditional family values, the problem of the family are often better handled by the right because the family itself tends to be elevated as a problem and named outright (Willis, 2014). In this way, the left gets hamstrung in the debate about the family, unable to exert an opinion about the family from any moral point of view, that is, the left lacks the language to discuss the family as a vector of social problems and struggles and thus ends up incapable of offering solutions to the problems that face the family. We examine this dynamic in the concluding chapter, where we begin to move from a paradox of liberation toward a dialectic of liberation.

The critique of the neoliberal family that Melinda Cooper (2017) presents will argue something very close to what we argued thus far. However, Cooper does not discuss the psychic and libidinal dimension of the politics surrounding the neoliberal family. This book can be considered, in small part, as an effort to contribute to that missing dimension of Cooper's wonderful argument. Cooper (2017) rightly argues that the liberal and conservative crisis over the family largely resulted in a wider compact and agreement at the level of policy, and the neoliberal family is thus not a left or a right-wing phenomenon. Today's family is shaped by capitalist imperatives more than by ideological or grassroots movements of either the right- or left-wing.

A critical example of the complicity between right- and left-wing liberal politicians over the family is found in the French political and civic culture during the mid to late twentieth century, just as the early onset of finance capital began to dawn in the early 1970s (Robcis, 2013). In this context, psychoanalysis was deployed as a scientific and academic weapon used by politicians and the legal community to preserve the family and its attendant state protections, more precisely, to shelter the family from marketization. As the family was placed at the very center of neoliberal reforms in America and Britain under Thatcher and Reagan; French politicians, both conservative and liberal, deployed psychoanalytic accounts of the family, particularly the work of Jacques Lacan and the anthropologist Claude Lévi-Strauss, to provide support against the marketization of the family (Robcis, 2013, pp. 18–20).

Unlike Cooper's analysis of the American political consensus that sought a further precarity of the family—meant to accelerate the deterioration of the welfare state in the rise of neoliberalism—Robcis' analysis shows how the cross-partisan consensus in France elevated a more conservative defense of the family and utilized psychoanalysis and structuralism to protect the stability and dignity of the family. For French liberal and conservative policymakers, Lacan's thought lent credence to the view that the "symbolic law" must be strengthened in the face of the marketization of everyday life. This process was explicitly interpreted as "Americanization" (Robcis, 2013, p. 219).[10]

Camille Robics has argued (2013) that the reception of psychoanalysis and structuralism in French social and political life in the mid-to-late twentieth century brought with it a conservative reaction in the form of an argument for "familialism" within French Republicanism more generally (Robcis, 2013). But ultimately, Robics shows how the deployment of familialist arguments distorted the teachings of structuralism and Lacanian thought by claiming that structures such as the Oedipus complex point to the necessity to strengthen the symbolic, which was in decline, according to these arguments, because of the withering of the institution of the family brought on by unchecked American liberalism, homosexual marriage, in vitro fertilization, and the erosion of welfare state protections (Robcis, 2013, pp. 235–236).

Although we are placing the paradox of liberation at the very center of our study, we are not offering up a pessimistic appraisal of the political role of the family in the contemporary conjecture by arguing that liberation is fundamentally stunted or inevitably reproduces its own self-defeat. On the contrary, we consider a range of proposals for radically transforming the family, including family abolition, which comes out of socialist-feminist

---

[10] Lacan in *Seminar VII* speaks of the American way: "Here the question of different goods' is raised in their relation to desire. All kinds of tempting goods offer themselves to the subject; and you know how imprudent it would be for us to put ourselves in a position of promising the subject access to them all, to follow the American way." It is nevertheless the possibility of having access to the goods of this world that determines a certain way of approaching psychoanalysis—what I have called "the American way." "It also determines a certain way of arriving at the psychoanalyst's and making one's demand" (p. 219).

and Marxist thought. Finally, we speculate in the conclusion about how to grapple with the paradox of liberation and conceive of new political and experimental organizations of the family that might get us out of the neoliberal family and all its precarity and exhaustion.

Our aim is to extend an olive branch to radical orientations and liberation movements by asking how the paradox of liberation might re-open the question that concerned Wilhelm Reich: why do people fight for their servitude as if it was their liberation?

In Deleuze and Guattari's reading of this Reichian conundrum, they argue that it is desire and its relation to an Oedipalized sremus that produces this repressive tendency. For Deleuze and Guattari, people desire their own servitude because the social relations have imposed constraints on the unconscious that tether and tie subjects to repressive relations. The paradox of liberation takes this insight but draws out its consequences at the collective level, showing that *any liberatory moment or rupture will face the collapse of ego ideals, and an attendant socialization of the superego will restrain that movement.*

This is an insight from psychoanalysis that is meant for ethical and political realities. In the movement from liberation to emancipation lies the paradox of liberation. Toward this end, the concluding chapter will attempt to situate the political problems that emerge considering this paradox and how alternative communities on the left embody different superego figures that draw us toward a dialectics of liberation. The question we are thus faced with is how to forge a transformation of the neoliberal family form. This comes down to forging solidarities for political change, or what we can call furthering class struggle in Marxist terms. This means that any thinking of the transformation of the family must think the emergence of class struggle and the political is just that: the contestation over social antagonisms.

In an everyday sense, it is true that "everything is of the political." But in actuality the political is a rarer phenomenon that emerges in distinct moments of uprising, crisis, and patient political organization. The legacy of the cultural liberationist demands for the family's freedom and the possibility of a different form of the family are incredibly important demands that call for a more care-based organization of the family. Fulfilling these demands calls for political action. They also entail a commitment to furthering the 60's and 70's "revolution of everyday life," a project that requires patient networks of solidarity across class, race, and geographic barriers.

The cultural and the political antagonisms of our world meet up in the politics of the family, and politically our world is dominated by liberalism, which constrains the psychic binds of the family. We must understand that liberalism has a long history of an Oedipal problem, that is, the liberalist ideology has a theory of subjectivity. Liberalism does indeed present a means for resolving political contradictions, but its solutions are not adequate for furthering the cause of liberation and emancipation.[11]

The other guiding concept of this book is what we name the crisis of initiation, a tendency that plagues the condition of subjectivity (or, more colloquially, of "self-making"). The crisis of initiation is a concept that will function as a compass, pointing us toward understanding a subjective problem that is borne, in large part, from the effect of the hyper-marketization of everyday life. We discuss this subjective crisis from Lacan's perspective, and we aim to show how Lacan provides a historical periodization of the emergence of this crisis. Furthermore, Lacan offers an ethics for managing its effects at the level of belief and ideology. To navigate this crisis, we turn to two great philosophers of subjectivity, René Girard and Alain Badiou. We find that the project of emancipation (for Badiou) and the technology of religion and its rites (for Girard) are two avenues by which to think through this crisis.

This book is an invitation to think about the family anew, to think about the family at the intersection of liberation and emancipation. To think the family in such a way that we avoid reifying another model of the bourgeois family in our attempts to transform the family. How do we learn from historical sequences that sought liberation of the family while avoiding the sorts of capture they became entangled in? The bourgeois family form has always been premised on a profoundly unequal distribution of its promises. We must think a new family organization beyond the demands of labor and achievement, beyond the marketized and socialized family, and the insights of psychoanalysis will guide us in this effort.

---

[11] We use liberation and emancipation somewhat synonymously but one helpful way to conceive of the two concepts in this text is to consider liberation as those demands which concern the cultural revolution of everyday life and emancipation as the area of class struggle and politics, i.e., as the contestations that emerge from that struggle. In a sense emancipation is a more total form of freedom than liberation and in that way, emancipation connects to the 'universal' dimension more than does liberation, which sees itself as more localized to a given groups set of demands for freedom.

REFERENCES

Boltanski, L., & Chiapello, E. (1999). *The New Spirit of Capitalism* (G. Elliott, Trans.). Verso Books.

Cooper, M. (2017). *Family Values: Between Neoliberalism and the New Social Conservatism* (p. 16). Princeton University Press.

Davies, W. (2016). The New Neoliberalism. *New Left Review*, (121), 129.

Lasch, C. (1976). The Family as a Haven in a Heartless World. *Salmagundi, Skidmore College*, (35), 42–55.

Lasch, C. (1991). The Culture of Narcissism: American Life in An Age of Diminishing Expectations W.W. Norton & Co.

Piketty, T. (2013). *Capital in the Twenty First Century*. Harvard University Press.

Robcis, C. (2013). *The Law of Kinship: Anthropology, Psychoanalysis, and the Family in France*. Cornell University Press.

Weber, M. (2002). *The Protestant Ethic and the Spirit of Capitalism: And Other Writings* (1st ed.). Penguin Books.

Willis, E. (2014). *The Essential Ellen Willis*. University of Minnesota Press.

CHAPTER 2

The Family Spirit and Social Reproduction

Abstract This chapter begins with a discussion of how the bourgeois family invented a distinct mode of exchange that differentiated the family from other forms of wage labor. It looks at how the bourgeois family endows the family with the illusion of its own private existence, or "family spirit" by using Pierre Bourdieu's theory of "symbolic exchange." We examine Marx and Engels's critique of the bourgeois family and socialist-feminist critiques of the family, which extend this analysis even further. We end this chapter with an analysis of the legacy and contemporary role of socialist-feminist critiques of the family and some of the challenges and contradictions abolitionists face today when the "care network" of the family has been so thoroughly marketized.

Keywords Social reproduction • Family spirit • Pierre Bourdieu • Socialist-feminism • Symbolic exchange • Neoliberalism

We think we know what a family is when we invoke its name; the very idea of the family possesses a profound "common sense." But what accounts for the common sense of the family? To answer this question is to begin to crack open the ambiguous status of the family as split between a supposed private, sealed-off existence *and* the fact that the family is also a primary vector for the social reproduction of the capitalist social order. In this

© The Author(s), under exclusive license to Springer Nature Switzerland AG 2022
D. Tutt, *Psychoanalysis and the Politics of the Family: The Crisis of Initiation*, The Palgrave Lacan Series,
https://doi.org/10.1007/978-3-030-94070-6_2

chapter, we begin by discussing how this family spirit, or common sense, emerges. That is, how does the illusion of the family's separateness from social reproductive processes become a common sense in everyday life? To answer this question, we turn to the ideological function of the family as developed by the French sociologist Pierre Bourdieu's theory of symbolic exchange. We then open the other side of the family—the social reproductive function of the family—by looking at Hegel's and later Marx's critique of the family, which aims to resolve this split status of the family.

For Hegel, the family is arguably the most important locus for developing his more comprehensive theory of socially grounded freedom and individuality. We then turn to the socialist-feminist and the Marxist tradition, which emerges from the Hegelian perspective but turns the problematic on its head. The Marxist-feminist critique of the family places the family at the very center of a wider analysis of social reproductive labor, exploitation, and gendered hierarchy. This tradition demands nothing less than an overcoming—*sublation*[1]—or abolition of the bourgeois family form.

There is perhaps no better example of ideology, defined here as the ways that beliefs legitimate the power of a class or group, than the ideology found in the common sense we assign to the family. We know that the family is at the very core of reproduction strategies: succession across generations, fertility, and matrimonial strategies, economic and educational strategies, but through these processes, a certain logic emerges that binds a more common idea of the family as separate from these very strategies. One way to describe this ideology is that it operates on a disavowal mechanism. It discards its complicity in the other scene of social reproduction and, in so doing, affirms its separate status and common sense. The common sense of the family transcends its members, like "a transpersonal person endowed with a common life and spirit and a particular vision of the world" (Bourdieu, 1998, p. 65). We tend to experience the family as a spirit, as a uniqueness that is both symbolic, biological and cultural. It is a curious fact that the business of genealogy and blood tests for ancestry are booming.[2]

---

[1] When Marx and Engels propose the abolition of the family in the *Communist Manifesto*, the term used is "Aufheben," the famous German word which maintains several contradictory meanings, "to lift up," "to abolish," "cancel" or "suspend," or "to sublate." The term has also been defined as "abolish," "preserve," and "transcend."

[2] The interest in genealogy is in large part a result of the advancements in the ease, cost, and accessibility of DNA testing of one's ancestry. What this fascination signifies is above all

We tend to experience the family as a shelter, for without a well-fortified illusion of the family's lack of complicity with social reproduction, the very meaning of the family would fray at the edges. This space of the family spirit is one where a different logic of exchange is at work, a logic that is distinct from the exchange value in which capitalism operates. In Bourdieu's analysis of the family, he calls this the logic of "symbolic exchange." At the heart of this logic is a taboo that is made on making explicit the otherwise transparent calculative and utilitarian rationales that are typically at play in capitalist exchanges. Instead, the family spirit and the common sense of the family is made possible through acts of symbolic exchange that take place in the family day-in-and-day-out: gifts imparted to children for education, the housewife working unwaged house labor, and so on.

These forms of symbolic exchange make up the *rites of the family* and the maintenance of this spirit; from paying for the education of its members to the daily time that is voluntarily given to personal improvement and enrichment, to the negotiation of sibling rivalry within the family, Bourdieu writes "symbolic exchange is an alchemy that transforms the truth of relations of domination in paternalism" (Bourdieu, 1998, p. 98). The family is thus the elementary form of symbolic exchange in contradistinction to capitalist calculation and utilitarian maximization that dominates most forms of exchange in the world. However, for the family spirit to maintain its efficacy as separate from social reproduction, there must be a taboo to make the utilitarian logic underneath symbolic exchange *too explicit*. The family spirit is thus in tension with marketization and sees marketization as a threat from the outside. In this way, the family has a hostile and ambivalent tension with capitalist social reproduction.

A major effect of the "hyper-marketization" of the family today is that the taboo on making explicit these calculative and utilitarian logics is no longer capable of maintaining the same ideological efficacy. Yet it is important to note that there is no one homogenous family and that not all families experience this deterioration of symbolic exchange. The class system does not evenly distribute the possibility for symbolic exchange within

else an interesting shift in the foreclosure of the mystery of one's ancestors, an insight which can be thought of in relation to Lacan's thesis that there is today a decline in initiation. When the secret of the family spirit is not only revealed in its naked complicity with the market and in the illusion of the transparency of one's genetic relation to ancestors, this signals a mutation in the status of knowledge and even of unconscious knowledge of the family.

families. How does a working-class family function differently, for example? How does a family subjected to more stringent labor routines, lacking free time, leisure, and inherited wealth treat symbolic exchange?

In a capitalist society, it is the bourgeois family that sets the ideal mold of the family, and one of the things that marks the neoliberal period is the profound deterioration of the efficacy of this private bourgeois family. Even the middle class is stretched thin in its capacity to reproduce the rites of symbolic exchange. Consider the housewife who has no material utility or price credit. They are excluded from the market taboo of calculation. Her labor is only sanctioned by "feeling" and by the closed system of recognition that labor may, or may not, be received from the family. This voluntary labor is an example of the idea of the "taboo on making it explicit" in that this labor has no formal means to seek a wage or be properly recognized outside of the privacy of the family.

It is important to mention in this context that a major strategy of '60s–'70s-era socialist-feminist political organizing included the movement known as "Wages for Housework," which sought out political demands for the eradication of this taboo and for the liberation of women's labor to be recognized politically and socially.[3] We can understand the working-class family as tending to possess a far less ideological relation to the family spirit. A different form of realism about the family spirit pervades the working-class family; that is, its members are aware of the sacrifices it takes to reproduce the family. They are aware that the ends it serves to reproduce the family are not of the family's making.

What is essential, psychoanalytically speaking, about the "family spirit" is that it transcends its members and endows the family with a common life and spirit. Without this ideology afforded by symbolic exchange, that is, afforded by a separate logic of exchange to that of the market, the family could not produce or dispense ego ideals of tradition and reproduce its distinct familial rites and practices. The cultivation of the family spirit is thus a sort of training ground for each of its members to apply the family spirit outside the family. Importantly, the family spirit is transferred to the workplace, the corporate setting, the school, and other institutions. A breakdown in the family spirit spells a breakdown in trust in institutions and a breakdown in what Bourdieu calls the "alchemy" of the symbolic

---

[3] One of the most articulate spokespeople for this vein of socialist-feminist organizing is Silvia Federici, whose support for the *Wages for Housework* movement, founded in 1972, stands out as a testament to the ongoing struggle for women's liberation from the household.

exchange necessary to forge this idea of belonging in other areas of work and communal life. According to Bourdieu, the family is an "archetypal model for all social groups, functioning as a corporate body." In short, the family spirit is a crucial concept to understand our wider argument in this book as it is the family spirit which is the relay system from the family outward to institutions.

The fantasy of the bourgeois family sheltered from social reproduction is based on the efficacy of its neutral and *disinterested* space of symbolic exchange. Thus, the only way the bourgeois family, which is the family form that every family is forced to live up to, even the working-class family, stakes out a spirit all its own is by adopting symbolic exchange protocols. Neoliberalism is marked by laws and policies that aim to strengthen the bourgeois family as a vector of private wealth and power via relaxed taxation on family inheritance and a general paternalization of institutions. For example, the rise of in loco parentis laws on colleges and universities that enforce the idea that colleges should act "in the place of the parent"—responsible not just for the student's education but also for their physical and *moral safety* have risen to the norm of campus culture across America.

These laws on college campuses—that emerged as an outgrowth of the '60s and '70s culture wars in California—do not consider students as complete adults, nor do they consider them as children. College students are treated with an ambivalent paternalism where their agency and responsibility are tethered to a paternal source whether they have that source of support or not. College and university culture has thus become an even more intensified zone for paternalism, and Cooper (2017) suggests that one of the effects of these laws is that revolts to "the system" tend to now take the form of more *intimate revolt*. As a result, there is a breakdown of the family spirit while the neoliberal policy changes have made more and more institutions in loco parentis.

The family spirit in neoliberalism has gone beyond the private, bourgeois family and a more pervasive sense of paternalism permeates our institutions. Bourdieu's analysis of the family reveals a split dynamic within the family, wherein the real dimension of social reproduction is covered over by the taboo on making the reproductive social labor explicit. But there are exceptions to this taboo, such as the housewife who performs labor that breaks the taboo on making market logics explicit by offering up a different logic of exchange, namely, through a logic grounded in affect and feeling. The housewife points to the *real dimension of social reproduction* at the family's heart, the part that its members otherwise disavow. But there are entire families, working-class families to be exact, which are composed of the housewife's labor, where the taboo on making explicit is not feasible.

The ideological composition of this family spirit that Bourdieu located in the bourgeois family has its origins in the Protestant Reformation. The writings of John Calvin grant the family a definite function: through subjection to the rule of the family, a man prepares himself for types of subjection in society that are more difficult to bear. Similarly, Martin Luther (2010) writes: "Their (the parents) condition or defect does not deprive them of their due honor. We must not regard their persons as they are, but the will of God, who ordered and arranged things thus" (Luther, p. 52).

Another significant theoretical insight into the family comes from Hegel, who theorizes the family as the ethical root of the state. For Hegel, the family brings out characteristics through which the individual can become a part of the state, representing objective morality. As Herbert Marcuse writes (2008), for Hegel, the family "is the first, still direct and natural form of the objective universality which supersedes 'subjective particularity'; it is the ethical spirit in its immediate and natural form." Hegel tied the "substantial personality" of the family to property and argued that only through the family is property no longer made arbitrary. Hegel's theory of the family is undoubtedly grounded in a theory of freedom that relies upon an elaborate set of social relations to actualize freedom as such. As Hegel writes in *Phenomenology of Spirit*, "the end and content of what [the individual family member] does and actually is, is the family" (Hegel, 1977, p. 451). As David Ciavatta (2009) writes:

> On Hegel's account, the familial sphere lays claim to being a unified, concrete whole unto itself that does not ultimately draw its ethical authority from a normative sphere that extends beyond its own interiority; rather, the nature of this sphere is such that it enables the particular familial relationships that constitute it to be experienced as self-sufficient, self-determined ethical authorities in themselves. (p. 57)

Marx and Engels's writings on the origins of the bourgeois family provide an important corrective to the origins of the private bourgeois family that we have discussed thus far. The Marxist and later socialist-feminist analysis of the family pulls the imaginary rug of symbolic exchange out from under its feet, leaving us face-to-face with an understanding of the family as a vector of social reproduction. In turning to the Marxist and socialist-feminist analysis of the family, we aim to open a new periodization of the "socialization of the family" we explored in the opening chapter. Engels' *The Origin of the Family, Private Property and the State* (Engels, 2000) brings out an important anthropological focus to the origin of the bourgeois family by noting that prior to the bourgeois family, tribal structures were often matriarchal; and the bourgeois family is a distinct patriarchal formation (2000). This critique has proven to be highly influential to later socialist-feminist interpretations and critiques of the family, although many socialist-feminists wage critique of Engels, for which more later.

What is the Marxist critique of the family? Let us answer this question with reference to the theory of the value-form under capitalism. Since capital constantly expands to produce more value, in this expansion, capital destroys social links and social bonds that, almost paradoxically, make the loss of those connections feel ever-more crucial. Capitalism does pose a break with the social bonds of feudalism and through enclosure and accumulation of capital it destroyed the various communities that were central to human social existence to make way for an economy in which man himself was the aim of production (Camatte, 2006).

Marxist theory argues that capitalism can only develop on condition that it frees the laborer by making him into a commodity, but to do so, capital destroys the various communities which had encompassed the laborer, which were governed, in a debased way, by an economy in which man was the aim of production. What capitalism thus offers is a replacement community, what Marx calls the "material community" (2006), which is required to overcome the human fragmentation that comes with the reduction of individuals to a set of exchanges. Capital thus presents an alternative community to the pre-capitalist "natural community." As the Marxist theorist Jacques Camatte (2006) notes:

> The individual has not produced as a member of a "natural community," and yet through exchange and the division of labour, his product becomes social. He owes the possibility of appropriating a product not to participation in a community, but rather to the fact that he himself has produced one too. This is the beginning of the material community created by means of production, or, more exactly, by means of its products. A community like this can no longer result from the uniting or reuniting of men, but from that of things, while at the same time it must also stabilize bonds between them. (p. 101)

Marx does not posit a romantic notion of a natural community that the communist revolution will restore. To the contrary, Marx writes of the "social individual" in the *Grundrisse* and remarks that as capital reaches a post-industrial form of maturity, the specific social dimension of life will come to dominate and set the preconditions for a communist social order. In this way, Marx is opposed to any nostalgic longing for a return to a more stable community arrangement and, by extension, the family. Although, in Marx's later work, he provides an account of post-industrial capitalism that reveals an important double bind that faces the family: just as "all that is solid melts into air," this withering of social, familial, and civil bonds results in a general socialization of individuality. In other words, Marx shows that post-industrial capitalism is a steady saga of the socialization of the material community and the fragmentation of the natural community that had already been steadily torn apart in industrial capitalism. This insight presents a paradoxical site of freedom for the family: as the socialization of reproduction intensifies in post-industrial capitalism. Eli Zaretsky's (1976) history of the family provides an important corrective to how the bourgeois family was molded and ultimately shaped by the working class. He argues:

> For those reduced to proletarian status from the petty bourgeoisie, one's individual identity could no longer be realized through work or through the ownership of property – individuals now began to develop the need to be valued for themselves . . . . The family became the major sphere of society in which the individual could be foremost – it was the only space the proletarians "owned." Within it, a new sphere of social activity began to take shape – personal life. (p. 61)

The invention of the bourgeois family in the early nineteenth century put forth the promise of the family as a haven, a private space sheltered away from society. But this private sphere of the family was not, and has never been, an evenly distributed promise. Zaretsky's historical analysis shows that the class antagonisms implicit in capitalist societies led to a situation in which the proletarian family experienced the family as the only space in society where the individual could be valued "for itself." In other words, the need for the individual to be valued "for itself" arises with man's dominance turned into a commodity on the market. In this alienating situation, the family emerges as the only space exempt from the subjugation to value. This insight adds a new layer of complexity to the wider socialist-feminist tradition that insists on family abolition centered on a praxis of the working class.

The contradiction at play here is that the working class finds the family a haven in capitalist society despite the profound constraints they face in re-producing the bourgeois family and its family spirit which shelters the members of the family from the demands of labor. This contradiction has been a hallmark of capitalist social life since the invention of the bourgeois family and it has only intensified in more recent neoliberal family structures as the family is now overworked and even more precarious. For the working class especially, the family remains the primary, if not the only, locus where the self can be valued for itself.

Consider the way Margaret Thatcher (1987), one of the chief political operators and architects of the neoliberal era, situated the family. In Thatcher's by now infamous statement, "there is no such thing as society," we often forget how central the family is to Thatcher's vision of an ideal social order:

> [T]hey are casting their problems on society and who is society? There is no such thing! There are individual men and women and there are families and no government can do anything except through people and people look to themselves first... *There is no such thing as society.* There is living tapestry of men and women and people and the beauty of that tapestry and the quality of our lives will depend upon how much each of us is prepared to take responsibility for ourselves and each of us prepared to turn round and help by our own efforts those who are unfortunate. (Keay, 1987)

The "they" referenced here are those citizens who believe the government has a role in tying individuals together in some sort of common social pact. For Thatcher, society must be replaced by relations of individuals held together by self-interest, each taking responsibility for their own sphere of property, profit, and ultimately of value. Thatcher's sentiment fulfills Marx's argument we discussed above that there is an intensification of the "social individual" in post-industrial capitalism and this affects the family because the family is more thoroughly socialized and tasked with far more demands for ensuring the reproduction of the social order.

The family in neoliberal life is thus tasked with the impossible duty to provide stability it cannot possibly fulfill, namely, to serve as the receptacle laboring unit for the absent welfare state and its attendant social services. Thus, today, the family finds itself called upon to absorb roles formerly delegated to the state in this new arrangement of the neoliberal society, which means that the family is thrown to an even more socialized form of existence.

Marxist-feminist theory (2015) and socialist-feminist thought draws a great deal of insight from the Marxist analysis of the family. Still, it throws into question whether Marxism, particularly Engels's work on the family, can adequately challenge the ideological construction of femininity and masculinity that tends to "cling to a romantic conception of heterosexual love as the basis of a new, 'socialist' family'" (McIntosh and Barrett, p. 18). The socialist-feminist critique narrows in on the fact that the insight we have sought to bring to the table in this chapter, namely, that the "private" social life of the bourgeois family remains the primary site where gendered and patriarchal hierarchy is naturalized. Thus, gendered and patriarchal violence is also at play in the act of symbolic exchange and the taboos of the family's private existence. This makes for a concealed oppression of the family under what are often cruel and brutal relations of gendered and patriarchal domination.

Therefore, the Marxist-feminist tradition is skeptical of the proposal that a socialist family form, as distinct from a bourgeois family form, would itself re-set hierarchies of patriarchal power. In the socialist-feminist thought of Sheila Rowbotham, Angela Davis, and Juliet Mitchell, three preeminent authors in this tradition, the family in capitalist societies is understood to be at the very heart of the reproduction, not only of "social" reproduction but also of relations of power that sustain social inequalities. For this tradition of thought, the inequalities of family life function as ground zero for the *normalization and naturalization of a society of extreme economic, racial, and gender inequality and hierarchy.*

We must retain these insights into our broader argument of the family spirit because patriarchal domination is what can go into the family spirit but does not always have to go into it. These authors pinpoint the problem of labor within the intimate and so-called private domain of the family that women are expected to perform, without a wage and form a radical political praxis from that basis that the taboos on making this labor explicit and recognized, compensated, and so on, requires a political revolution. It is essential to understand that without the unwaged sacrifice of labor, the family—and mostly women—perform for the capitalist system, capitalism would be incapable of self-reproducing. Thus, the abolition of the family is conceived as a central tenet of revolutionary praxis in socialist-feminist thought.

The legacy of family abolition, from the *Communist Manifesto* of 1848 all the way up to the present, is a tradition of practice and political militancy. In the era of neoliberalism, the abolitionist position faces several built-in challenges to its praxis and demands: the working class in the post-2008 restructuring of the economy has itself produced an economy of marketized care networks. The "gig economy" from apps to share personal homes, to offer transportation with one's personal car, to all sorts of other everyday labor "side hustles" poses a grave threat to the implicit care-based demands of the abolitionist movement.

The "sharing economy" lauded by Silicon Valley and corporate America stretches workers thin, depriving the working class of leisure time as it demands that workers supplement their day jobs with extra side hustle work. The sharing economy is a highly socialized structure, calling on workers to provide transportation, to open their homes to others and perform tasks for other families such as grocery shopping. This gig economy arose following the 2008 economic recession and it stands out as an example of what Marx saw as a main tendency of post-industrial capitalism, namely an intensified socialization of labor. In the concluding chapter, we will discuss the gig economy and its effect on the contemporary family. One of its paradoxes is that its organization is effectively horizontal and care-based. Thus, for Marxist-feminists this socialized form of economy provides a possible basis by which to more thoroughly socialize the family. It is important that we understand the different ways that communists are today (2021) raising demands for family abolition. Several new works place the praxis of family abolition back on the table for communist organizing.[4]

As M.E. O'Brien (2019), a communist theorist, points out, "the family, particularly the heterosexual nuclear family, has served as the dominant and most stable mode of generational reproduction for proletarians under capitalism" (p. 414). This chapter has sought to understand the ideological function of the family that keeps it tethered to social reproduction. We now turn in the next chapter to understand the psychic politics more fully at work in the family, that is, what are the subjective and the psychic effects of this intensified socialization of the family. These are the questions that concern us.

---

[4] It is important to mention the creative proposal of Sophie Lewis in *Full Surrogacy Now: Feminism Against Family* (2021), who advocates for the expansion of surrogacy networks for childrearing that completely abandon nuclear and heteronormative family structures. Lewis bases much of this proposal on the example of surrogacy centers in India. We will not comment or critique this work directly here, however, we hope that the concepts and arguments we derive in this text pertaining to the psycho-politics of the family might create a conversation with the abolition tradition.

REFERENCES

Bourdieu, P. (1998). *Practical Reason*. Stanford University Press.

Camatte, J. (2006). *Capital and Community: The Results of the Immediate Process of Production and the Economic Work of Marx* (D. Brown, Trans.). Pattern Books.

Ciavatta, D. (2009). *Spirit, the Family, and the Unconscious in Hegel's Philosophy.* State University of New York Press.

Cooper, M. (2017). *Family Values: Between Neoliberalism and the New Social Conservatism*. Princeton University Press.

Engels, F. (2010). *Origin of the Family, Private Property, and the State* (Alick West, Trans.). London: Penguin Books.

Hegel, G. (1977). *Phenomenology of Spirit* (A. Miller, Trans.). Oxford University Press.

Keay, D. (1987, September 23). *Interview for Woman's Own ("No Such Thing as Society")*. See https://www.margaretthatcher.org/document/106689

Lewis, S. (2021). *Full Surrogacy Now: Feminism Against Family*. Verso Books.

Luther, M. (2010). *Luther's Primary Works* (K. Buchheim, Trans.). Nabu Press.

Marcuse, H. (2008) *Studies on Authority* (Joris De Bres, Trans.) Verso Books.

McIntosh, M., & Barrett, M. (2015). *The Anti-Social Family*. Verso Books.

O'Brien, M. (2019). *Endnotes Volume 5: The Passions and The Interests*. Endnotes.

Zaretsky, E. (1976). *Capitalism, the Family and Personal Life*. Harper & Row.

CHAPTER 3

The Social Superego and the Paradox of Liberation

Abstract This chapter analyzes the composition of the social superego, the predominant form of the superego under late capitalism. It looks specifically at the political basis of Freud's discovery of the superego and how Freud's concepts, from Oedipus, death drive to the superego, must each be read with an explicitly political context in mind. It then turns to the work of Étienne Balibar and Kojin Karatani and apply their analysis of the Freudian superego to understand the way this concept changes more fully in moments of uprising political instability and crisis, and how through this reading we can understand late capitalism as a time that is superego deprived. With this understanding of the superego in mind, we gain better insight into the paradox of liberation and how superegoic dynamics play into politics.

Keywords Social superego • Freud • Oedipus • Psychoanalysis and politics • Kojin Karatani • Death drive • Late capitalism

Our argument thus far is that the intensification of labor demands on men and women alike, the rise of expert managers over the sphere of everyday life, from the gig economy to smartphones and apps that manage

© The Author(s), under exclusive license to Springer Nature
Switzerland AG 2022
D. Tutt, *Psychoanalysis and the Politics of the Family: The Crisis of
Initiation*, The Palgrave Lacan Series,
https://doi.org/10.1007/978-3-030-94070-6_3

household life, have all created dynamics within the family of hyper-marketization. This hyper-marketization is also a disciplinary system. Indeed, the neoliberal order is—post-2008—a "punitive" social order that enforces debt peonage, austerity, and anti-socialist politics to punish and discipline its citizenry, especially the working class. The post-2008 period has also been marked by revolts against this punitive order, from the rise of protest movements on the left such as Occupy Wall Street and Black Lives Matter (Taylor, 2016) to right populism and neofascism.[1] How does the family undergoing this more ubiquitous *marketization of everyday life* cope with these dynamics, and what are the superegoic dimensions at play within the family today?

As we saw in the last chapter, the working-class family latches onto the family with ambivalence and passionate attachment, even though its promise are only partial. This has remained a feature of working-class family life: latching onto the family as the only refuge in a world of exploitation and labor and this continues today. Eli Zaretsky's analysis of the working-class family of the nineteenth century and early twentieth century reveals that although the promises of the private bourgeois family were never fully realizable, the family form itself—which takes the bourgeois form as its sole model—was nonetheless the primary locus of a singular subjective experience. Working-class people derived a sense of value in itself through the institution of the family, and the neoliberal family only extends this crisis to more subjectivities.

In Lasch's argument, marketization causes the "ego ideals" of parents and caretakers transmitted to children to be profoundly destabilized. Today, this has led to identifications outside of the family via external technology mechanisms from apps to smartphones, and via institutions to become more in crisis. This has given rise to a new configuration of the superego, a more anonymous form of social authority, untethered from ideals; this is what we name the social superego.

For Lasch, the Fordist period was generally one wherein the ego ideals of the family, of one's network of teachers, and of immediate personal relations formed "ego ideals" out of which an institutional field then linked

---

[1] It is important to understand the origins of Black Lives Matter as a movement that arose in response to police violence against black citizens and which was also arising in the context of punitive neoliberalism and the overreach of the local state apparatus policing the black citizenry to fine, ticket and derive more revenue to compensate for the absence of welfare state support. For more on this interpretation of Black Lives Matter, see Taylor 2016, chapter 6.

up "ideal ego" identification with its order. The social order was thus capable of dispensing a superegoic mechanism that was also grounded on these institutions, including the family. What this theory of ideals through identification gets at is a wider psychoanalytic theory of recognition and the central importance of recognitive mechanisms in subjective life. As we will see in our turn to Lacan's theory of the ideals, this model of thinking ideals that Lasch works with has built-in theoretical flaws because it tends to consider ego-ideals-to-ideal-ego identifications along with a stable/unstable perspective. This leads to a moderate and even conservative reading of subjectivity because the more ideal order is the one that can bring psychic stability back to the table. A more liberatory approach aims to think about the revolution and fundamental transformation of the structures that sustain the unjust and constrained system.

To state our argument directly: under conditions of hyper-marketization, family subjectivity experiences the rise of a different form of the superego. This is a crueler and more aggressive form of superego because it lacks the same relay system to ideal egos in institutions and more local vectors of family and community life. There is thus a certain cynicism and ironic distance in how people believe in and relate to institutions that is concurrent to this hyper-marketization. In these conditions, *the superego is strengthened in direct proportion to the depletion and the diminishment of the efficacy of ego ideal identifications* (Lasch, 1991, p. 12). The social superego is a mediating force, and in what follows, we aim to discuss its effects and how it comes into existence.

The rise of the social superego gives way to a different form of self-making, which for Lasch meant that secondary narcissism—or pathological narcissism—is released as a normalized form of social personality. In other words, narcissism breaks down and undergoes a crisis wherein more pathological forms of "secondary narcissism" become more common: aggressive identifications instead of self-love tend to be the more dominant form of mediation of ideals. Primary narcissism for Freud is akin to Spinoza's conatus or the necessity of striving and self-preservation. In general, narcissism is marked by a libidinal form of self-love that is sexualized. Lasch replaced the Oedipus complex with the "Narcissus Myth" as the guiding form of subjective life in the early neoliberal period. In so doing, he pointed to this subjective shift in the process of primary narcissism, more precisely, to a pervasive stunting of primary narcissism. This stunting is directly correlated to the socialization of the family and the increasing dominance of the market intervening in more and more areas of individual psychic life.

Socially determined ego-ideal and ideal-ego identifications break down in this situation of pervasive "pathological narcissism," and the subject perceives the rules of the game in terms of the superego, not the ideal ego grounded in more concrete social relations that are less hampered by capitalist marketization.[2] There was thus a certain reprieve or distance from marketizing logics within the family prior to the rise of this hyper-marketization that meant subjects could manage authority more thoroughly; that is, they could more adequately work through the paternalistic identifications that are constitutive of any family structure. The breakdown of stable ego ideals is what leads to the emergence of the irrational and cruel pre-Oedipal archaic superego, that is, the "social superego." In this dynamic, the "social" becomes, as Simone Weil wrote, "the only idol," that is, the social envelops collective life in ways that are all-enveloping and suffocating (Weil, 1955, 117). We can thus understand Thatcher's dictum "there is no such thing as society" as giving way to the precise opposite reality. Everything is socialized, even the core of our psychic life.

The social superego's dominance over psychic life tracks with what the theorist Byung-Chul Han refers to as the "diminishment of the social other," an insight into how power operates in our society. Han argues from a philosophical, not exactly a psychoanalytic perspective that a diminishment of authority relations marks our society, and the very sphere of otherness has lost efficacy today. By "other," we mean here the same as ideal ego—the other of institutions, figures of authority, and so on: it is these figures that have lost their mediating hold over subjective life. In the wake of that loss the social superego emerges as a different logic of social compulsion and power, which puts constraints on working-through Oedipal dynamics. The social superego names something more anonymous source of authority at the core of the social; it is what emerges in the collapse of trust and commitment to the social itself. In Han's view, what Lasch calls the social superego is a feature of what he names the

---

[2] In *The Culture of Narcissism* (1979) Lasch frames the deeper theoretical framework of narcissism based on the idea of "pathological narcissism "which was refined and developed by the psychoanalyst Otto Kernberg. For a more detailed and thorough analysis of the role of Kernberg's ideas of pathological narcissism in Lasch's work, see Slavoj Žižek's early review essay of Lasch—Žižek 1986.

"achievement society." The "achievement society" or the "burnout society" are concepts that identify the ways in which neoliberal society are composed in distinction to the era of power and domination that preceded it.[3]

In Han's view, the injunction of the social superego and the ego ideals of institutions, the family and so on are internalized around an attitude of affirmation and hyper-positivity, whereas in the prior form of society, the superego was based on a prohibition model: the you "can" attitude reinforced the injunction of the you "should" attitude. But in the achievement society today, this injunction of the can/should is fully internalized and is no longer reliant on the social other. Injunctions toward pleasure, freedom, and inclination are no longer dependent on a *commanding other* that we had during the prior period which Han, tracking Foucault, refers to as the "disciplinary society" and locates in the late nineteenth century up to the rise of the Fordist period in the early 1900s. The achievement society produces a subject that lacks the sovereignty to declare its own singularity because it is not in a situation of domination and confrontation with an "other" that it must work-through, accept and or reject its authority. Authority has become a scandal to subjectivity because subjectivity is not routed through the same impasses with social others of authority. This condition is so total for Han that it signifies a collapse in the very basis of the Hegelian master-slave dialectic as a logic of social power.

Before we understand this internalization of power and the collapse of social otherness that emerges with the social superego, we need to investigate the companion concept to superego, namely, the Freudian theory of death drive. Freud's theoretical discovery of the death drive marks a shift in the way the superego relates to the social field; namely, in *Beyond the Pleasure Principle* (1920), aggression is thought of as a constitutive dynamic of the libidinal composition of the subject. The death drive is a theory that portends significant political consequences, which we will examine. Freud suggests that the death drive, this inward aggressivity, is mediated by the external dynamic of the superego, which he at times refers to as a "censor." But with the discovery of death drive the theory of the superego is now no longer mediated primarily by the censor mechanism,

---

[3] Han relies on the historical periodization of Gilles Deleuze and Michel Foucault, especially Deleuze's *Postscript on the Societies of Control*, an essay that first appeared in *L'Autre* journal, no. 1 (May, 1990). We discuss Deleuze's essay and theory of power in the chapter "The Political Stakes of the Social Superego."

it is dictated by the death drive. There is a political context and dynamic involved in Freud's discovery of the death drive just as there is an important political context involved with Freud's discovery of the Oedipus complex. We can't understand the core of psychoanalytic concepts without an understanding of the political dynamics that inform the development of its core concepts.

What is the death drive? Freud (2011) introduces the death drive in *Beyond the Pleasure Principle* (1920) as the "sadistic component in the sex drive" (Freud, p. 90). The death drive is thus the "original sadism" in the sexual drive and is also a source of unpleasure in the sexual drive that upsets the pleasure principle, or "a tendency serving a function whose task is to render the mental apparatus completely free of excitation, or to keep the amount of excitation in it constant or as low as possible" (p. 98). He argues the death drive precedes the pleasure principle and is not in a bound state. At times Freud refers to the drives in mythical terms calling it "demonic" in the sense that a demon is a pure figure of drive detached from the sexual drives. Freud writes, "the obscure anxiety of persons unfamiliar with analysis, who hesitate to awaken something they believe should be left asleep, is fundamentally a fear of the appearance of this demonic compulsion" (p. 75). This compulsion is discoverable in the repetition of dreams, the spontaneous play of children and in war traumatized patients in psychoanalysis.[4] But the demonic and masochistic status of the death drive is not the final word on the concept. The death drive is a theory not of death as such, it is a theory of the way inorganic matter is bound up with the drives. As Catherine Malabou (2007) puts it:

> What goes beyond and what comes back through to the compulsion to repeat is not the threat of death, not the image of endangered life, not the situation of a being-toward-death faced with her fragility. Such situations are not irreducible to pleasure. Freud would certainly have considered that the existential analysis developed in *Being and Time* would perhaps be able to supersede metaphysics, but not pleasure. What goes beyond the pleasure principle as the originary temporality is not the temporality of Dasein but the pure neutrality of inorganic matter. By pure neutrality, I mean a state of being which is neither life nor death but their very similarity. (p. 79)

---

[4] We discuss the famous "fort/da" game of Freud's grandson which is elaborated in *Beyond the Pleasure Principle* as an example of how the child masters the repetition compulsion in Chap. 5, "Oedipus: A Function of Initiation."

While there is much to be said about the death drive from a theoretical point of view, for our purposes, we will define it here as an internal source of negativity and aggression. The concept of the superego is developed most clearly in Freud's *The Ego and the Id* (1923), published three years after *Beyond the Pleasure Principle*. The superego is here defined as a part of the ego that internalizes the "moral character of the father" that is "under the influence of authority, religious teaching, schooling and reading" (p. 262). The superego regulates the "conscience" of the subject and under the conditions of the Oedipus complex, the superego internalizes the "unconscious guilt" of the child's parents.

With these summaries of the death drive and superego now fresh, we turn to understanding how there is an implicit dialectic between death drive and superego in Freud's thought. Freud's discovery of the death drive coincided with the political and social moment in Europe of the end of the Austro-Hungarian Empire following World War I. This was a time of profound social and political emancipation with the success of the Bolshevik Revolution, the collapse of the aristocratic regimes across Europe, including the Austro-Hungarian Empire and the Weimar regime where Freud was expanding psychoanalysis. The Marxist philosopher Kojin Karatani (2017) describes this moment in the following way:

> Freud, after *Beyond the Pleasure Principle*, albeit uncomfortably, attempted to reinforce culture, or the superego. It is not external control, but the aggressive drive itself that can inhibit the aggressive drive. By this thinking, he insisted on the necessity of maintaining the Weimar regime. It should be noted, however, that it was not the war itself but the patients who repeated the war every night that compelled Freud to take a drastic turn that changed the meaning of the superego and culture. Freud speculated that individuals should be cured of neurosis, but that states did not have to be cured of neurosis, namely culture. (p. 152)

Karatani rightly points out that Freud's great discovery of the death drive coincided with the collapse of the European aristocracy and that Freud was seeking a principle within his wider theoretical system to account for a stabilizing source for the subject experiencing a politically unstable social order. The time of Freud's Vienna was experiencing a liberationist upsurge in the wake of the Bolshevik Revolution of 1917 and the expansion of social democracy across central Europe. Freud was at the center of this profound liberationist moment in the former Austro-Hungarian Empire after World War I. He responded to this climate accordingly by promoting the expansion of "free clinics," a relaxation of the training system for new analysts, and a liberal transference theory. But while Freud embraced forms of socialistic egalitarian principles in the construction of the psycho-analytic clinic, the structure of Freud's close inner circle of psychoanalysts remained secretive and closed off.

Freud's liberal politics did indeed inform his theory of the superego, and the superego as a concept must be understood as a political concept. As Carl Schorske's influential essay on Freud's politics in *Fine-De-Siècle Vienna* (1961) argues, the political logic of Freud's moderate liberalism informed the development of his ideas even earlier than 1920. Schorske locates Freud's political commitments in the very discovery of the unconscious in *The Interpretation of Dreams*, published in 1899. Schorske provides essential political context to the Viennese political dynamics of the late nineteenth century, in which Freud, a Jewish intellectual facing ostracization and institutional marginalization, sought to rectify.

At the time, Europe was undergoing a revolutionary period and the class struggle was boiling up to the surface of political life. As a result, the traditional political dynamics were no longer "liberal versus conservative." The peasantry, the lower classes, and the working classes had attached to causes of socialism and nationalism, and the broader political spectrum was extraordinarily turbulent. Schorske argues that Freud's individual struggles for social recognition as a marginalized Jewish "scientist" forced Freud to move psychoanalysis beyond a merely scientific method toward an implicitly political one. But politics was founded for Freud, not on a revolt against the father, but on mediation and resolution with the father. In a fascinating juxtaposition of Freud's dream analysis of Rome in *The Interpretation of Dreams*, Schorske argues that the adoption of a scientific method of psychoanalysis was a way for Freud to put the Oedipal father at bay from the political entirely—and here we mean literally Freud's own attachments to his father—by making psychoanalysis a science Freud aimed to "lay the father's ghost" to rest in the field of politics (Schorske, 1981, p. 193).

In Freud's infamous "Revolutionary Dream" (1900), he analyzes a dream he had in which an aristocratic minister, Count Thun, is replaced with Freud's own father. In the dream, Freud is on a train, and he encounters the minister on the train. Freud confronts him and then flees his persecution, exiting the train and then all the sudden appearing on an academic campus. In the wake of this fleeing, Freud then returns to the train station to encounter a blinded man who he interprets as a stand-in for his own father, and he offers this man a urinal to pee. In his analysis of Freud's "Revolutionary Dream," Schorske (1981) points out that Freud neglects a more directly political reading of the significance of the dream. He states that it should be read as the origin of Freud's insistence that "patricide replaces regicide," that is, as the Freudian orientation to the political. As Freud (2017) recounts:

> The whole rebellious content of the dream, with its lèse majesté and its derision of the higher authorities, went back to rebellion against my father. A Prince is known as father of his country; the father is the oldest, first, and for children the only authority, and from his autocratic power the other social authorities have developed in the history of human civilization. (p. 150)

Many commentators, including the psychoanalyst Paul Verhaeghe (1998), have argued that in social terms, Freud's solution to politics is far from a mere "neutralizing" of politics, as Schorske suggests. By relying on the father to resolve the impasse of the political, Freud's politics "reinforces a phallocentric fascism, and the last version of this almost succeeded in exterminating his own people" (p. 88). But another way to read Freud's politics emerges when we examine the core of Freud's invention of the superego. Here we find the superego is structured on an antinomy: not only is it a mode of authority that can be made emancipatory or furthered in any given social order, but it also situates the subject in a "psychic tribunal." This double bind of the superego is found in the origin of the concept of superego itself, which emerges from two terms: "over," *Über*, and "compulsion," *Zwang*, which is inseparable from the law and especially the right to punish. Importantly, the superego is not equivalent to the Kantian concept of the "categorical imperative" as a structure of the unconscious. If it were, it would subordinate the subject to the law of morality.

To the law, the superego is paradoxically "co-occurring" as it both adheres and transgresses the law. The effect of this double bind is that the subject undergoes guilt. As Étienne Balibar (2017) writes, "how could the subject (the unconscious ego) not feel guilty of failing to reconcile what is both enjoined and prohibited?" (p. 243). The superego establishes a "tribunal" founded on a personal instance inscribed within a genealogical succession and an impersonal instance constituted by a network of institutions or apparatuses of domination and coercion, which includes the "family" comprising the point of intersection between these two. The family is the mediator of these two logics of the superego, which makes them effectively irrepresentable: "the superego, it's the family!" "The family, it's the superego!" (p. 249).

While the superego is transcribed and bound to a network of institutions that are often sources of domination and coercion, the "psychic tribunal" they establish should not be understood as creating conditions of voluntary servitude on the subject. To the contrary, the superego also connects the subject to the collective and to the community. Just as the superego's psychic tribunal situates the subject in a concrete communal instantiation between the network of domination and coercion, it also links the subject to an impersonal form of binding. Freud's 1928 essay on humor locates this more impersonal dimension of the superego and points to how it is not only an agency of repression and censorship.

To tease out this dual status of the superego, Freud contrasts humor with jokes, where humor functions with spontaneity and activeness—not with consciousness—whereas jokes function consciously. In making a humorous joke in comparison to a joke that uses wit and irony, we see the way this loop of the double bind functions both inside and outside to the connection of social relations. In other words, a humorous joke works on the level of nonsense and often incorporates bodily humor, as we find in the "Three Stooges." Furthermore, jokes rely on playing with consciousness, not the unconscious dimension of subjectivity. They use things like irony and wit to derive the funny moment or punchline, whereas humor relies on consciousness distortions, often not even relying on language.

In his analysis of the superego, Kojin Karatani draws out the distinction between humor and jokes and shows how this difference is homologous with the split with the binding that occurs in the superego. The critical difference here is between the conscious and unconscious dimensions of the superego: the binding to the network of authority brings on guilt, whereas the release from that binding tends to bring about shame. The superego is thus activated, in Karatani's reading, during moments of social and political crisis: revolt, uprisings, war. These moments of social turbulence tend to bring about a repressive intensification of superego dynamics, which we saw in the example of Freud's Vienna at the close of the nineteenth century. The political situation at that time was undergoing a form of class struggle, and the aristocratic order was struggling to retain its monopoly of authoritarian control. These moments of crisis give rise to the political, or a moment of heightened social antagonism, an idea which we examine in the chapter "The Political Stakes of the Social Superego."

However, just as social moments of change and transformation intensify superego dynamics among the citizenry, there are also periods in which the social order is *effectively without superego* and is governed primarily, although not exclusively, by the affect of shame. As Joan Copjec (2002) remarks, the affect of shame does not rely on the superego:

> Shame is awakened not when one looks at oneself, or those whom one cherishes, through another's eyes, but when one suddenly perceives a lack in the Other. At this moment the subject no longer experiences herself as a fulfillment of the Other's desire, as the centre of the world, which now shifts away from her slightly, causing a distance to open within the subject herself. This distance is not that "superegoic" one which produces a feeling of guilt and burdens one with an uncancelable debt to the Other, but is, on the contrary, that which wipes out the debt. In shame, unlike guilt, one experiences one's visibility, but there is no external Other who sees, since shame is proof that the Other does not exist. (p. 128)

With these insights into the superego, we can now understand the superego as a historically contingent feature of a given social order that is activated and transformed in concrete moments of social change and unrest. These moments give rise to and enforce superego dynamics, and different collectives—political movements, ideological orientations, and so on—develop distinctive superegoic tendencies which situate adherence to that group. Generally speaking, when superego forms emerge amid social unrest: war, crisis, revolution, and so on, the social order can expect conditions of guilt to predominate. There is an important dialectic of guilt and shame that is intrinsic to this dual status of the superego as we have outlined it.

As Balibar (2017) indicates, it is necessary that the radical "feeling of guilt" engendered by absolute coercion be "repressed and perpetuated, and along with it, the paradoxical equivalence of intentions and acts, behaviors of obedience and movements of transgression" (pp. 241–254). There is thus a need for the creation of a sphere of society in which superegoic effects can find a certain outlet that can spill over into a repository. The social order must contain an *other scene* by which the negative and anti-social affects of guilt can be granted a proper outlet. This insight tracks with Freud's "Radical Dream" in the *Interpretation of Dreams*. It shows that the birth or the emergence of the superego also spells the possibility of disabling the very repressive aspects of the superego at the same time. Karatani, in a way quite like Lacan, argues that shame is a dominant affect in the contemporary period. This means that capitalist consumerism and the social superego that it implies becomes the very means for the disabling of the other, more prohibitive form of superego that Freud discovered as a primarily political concept.

This insight also tracks well with Lacan's view in *Seminar XVII, The Other Side of Psychoanalysis* (1968–69), that shame primarily affects our current historical epoch.[5] Lacan argues that the rise of a "university discourse" dispenses shame as its core logic. According to Lacan, the university discourse is a bureaucratized form of social power that accelerates a great "shame at being alive." The university discourse is the "modern master's discourse," but unlike the master's discourse, it places the desire for knowledge at the root of its discourse. In the master's discourse, knowledge is produced by the slave and tied to *jouissance*, whereas in the university discourse, knowledge is bound to the master signifier S1. This master signifier comes in the form of the commandment to "keep on knowing"—the master occupies the half said, *le mi-dire de la verité* with this circulation. In the university discourse, one of the predominant modes of discourse in late-capitalist social life, the master is absent.

With this detour in understanding the superego's function as a political concept, we now return to our analysis of the social superego. We have argued the social superego emerges in the period of neoliberalism, mid-1970s to the present, and we now have a better means to understand the composition of the superego and how a more social form of the superego has arisen. The social superego does not suggest that the superego is somehow absent in the way Freud presents it. We instead claim that the superego should not be understood as a uniform phenomenon effecting all subjects in the same way. Furthermore, the social superego is an insight that is very much in line with Karatani's and Lacan's suggestion that late capitalism is indeed deprived of superego uniformity.

In our presentation of the "social superego" we have seen how it refers to the logic of superego in a social order in which patriarchal authority figures and ego ideals of the family and parents are no longer hegemonic

---

[5] As we examine in the following two chapters, Lacan periodizes the rise of the capitalist discourse in this context and there is a great deal of commonality with this periodization of the capitalist discourse and Karatani's argument that late capitalism is without superego. The late French philosopher Bernard Stiegler makes a similar argument to both thinkers and we consider that in the chapter "The Political Stakes of the Social Superego."

or the main organizing principle. We thus have a paradox emerge in this wider question of the "social" dimension of the superego. Suppose the superego is determined by an internal function of the death drive. In that case, the social dimension of the superego will persist even if the repressive censors of a predominantly patriarchal set of ego ideals lose their efficacy and decline. Thus, any social order undergoing a liberationist upsurge will still be confronted with superegoic mechanisms. More precisely, this is what we name the *paradox of liberation*. In fact, paradoxically, the collapse of ego ideals and instabilities of external censor mechanisms do not portend a collapse of superego but the necessity to acknowledge and work through its re-invention in the liberationist gesture itself.

To get at the heart of the social superego, we must locate its effects in the way subjects *believe* in the same command of its dictates. What distinguishes the break Lasch aptly points out, between the Fordist era of stable ego ideals to the rise of the social superego of neoliberalism, is how belief in the injunction serves as a pre-condition of the social superego. This point is illuminated by the anti-liberal polemicist and French intellectual Jean-Claude Michéa, who argues that today's superego is the bad mother: possessive and castrating. The superego functions in two forms: the first is to establish a disciplinary order of submission, and the second is to cede the desire of the subject. The maternal has no other way of expressing its devotion other than by "love and sacrificial devotion." Hence, the cruelty of the superego today resides in the ambiguous and necessary internalization of injunctions.

Instead of the same repressive "double bind" of the father's injunction in the prior era: "follow my advice, don't follow my advice," presenting a contradictory law, the contemporary period presents injunctions which follow a different logic: "you will visit your grandma, *and you will like it.*" There is thus an extra demand to internally act *as if* the subject conforms with the injunction itself. So, whereas the prior law of the father's double bind entailed a certain distance or breathing room from its injunction— effectively stating, "I don't care if you believe in what I say, just do it."[6] Today, the maternal superego requires the subject to take on their own personalization of the injunction; that is, the subject is incapable of relinquishing the very basis of the injunction residing within the power/command. This begs the question: if one party compels the other to adopt the

---

[6] This is a by now famous insight of Slavoj Žižek that builds off Lacan's general theoretical insight into the superego demand to enjoy, which he also locates as a historical shift.

injunction, have they really forced anyone to adopt anything, or have they *empowered* the subject to freely participate in the social superego? This internalization of the social superego establishes the basic disciplinary techniques of today's "achievement society." It is thus clearer now what Han means when he claims that the law today operates on an absence of the other.

With this analysis of the social superego, we can now see how the social superego is deprived of the same dual status of superego that was predominant in Freud's time. In Freud's superego, as we examined above, the binding of the subject to the social order brought on a predominant guilt in that attachment. Today, the social superego should not be understood as primarily maternal, as Michéa (2009) argues, but instead composed of an internalized form of injunction. In other words, the subject themselves must take up the legitimation of this injunction. Michéa will link this injunction as a disciplinary feature of the liberal bourgeois class order, even stretching back to the nineteenth century. His argument will resonate with our wider claims in the chapter "Liberalism and the Oedipal."

Where does this analysis of the social superego leave the family? In other words, if the family is the superego, and vice versa—in Freud's model of the superego—where is the family placed within the social superego? We argue the family is no longer the primary locus of superegoic training and enforcement, in large part because they don't have to be. There are, of course, exceptions to be noted here. In the analysis of American bourgeois family organization and training of children for meritocratic preparation, these superegoic dynamics are most definitely at play.[7] The social superego has largely, and quite effectively, displaced the prior role of the family as superegoic enforcer onto market mechanisms, resulting in a far more pervasive family structure to everyday institutions. It is not the cold mother that we must contend with and seek to work through, for such a figure is already a hyperbole. It is the fact that the social superego has such a ubiquitous presence today; it is everywhere and

---

[7] We do not spend too much time analyzing the bourgeois and middle-class professional practices of family rearing in this book, although for some very polemical and, at times, absurdly funny insights and anecdotes into the family dynamics of the professional managerial class, see Catherine Liu's *Virtue Hoarders: The Case Against the Professional Managerial Class*, Minnesota University Press, 2021.

nowhere at once. Its injunctions are effective because they don't need the family to enforce them.

REFERENCES

Balibar, E. (2017). *Citizen Subject: Foundations for Philosophical Anthropology.* Fordham University Press.

Copjec, J. (2002). *Imagine There is No Woman: Ethics and Sublimation.* MIT Press.

Freud, S. (1923). *The Ego and the Id.* The Standard Edition of the Complete Psychological Works of Sigmund Freud, Volume XIX (1923–1925): The Ego and the Id and Other Works, 1–66.

Freud, S. (2011). *Beyond the Pleasure Principle* (G. Richter, Trans. and T. Dufrense, Ed.). Broadview Press.

Freud, S. (2017). *Interpretation of Dreams* (A. Brill, Trans.). Digireads.com Publishing.

Karatani, K. (2017). *Nation and Aesthetics: On Kant and Freud.* Oxford University Press.

Lasch, C. (1991). *The Culture of Narcissism: American Life in an Age of Diminishing Expectations.* W. W. Norton & Company.

Malabou, C. (2007). Plasticity and Elasticity in Freud's Beyond the Pleasure Principle. *Diacritics, 37*(4), 79.

Michéa, J. (2009). *The Realm of Lesser Evil.* Polity Press.

Schorske, C. (1981). *Fine-De-Siècle Vienna, "Politics and Patricide in Freud's Interpretation of Dreams.".* Vintage Books.

Taylor, K.-Y. (2016). *From #BlackLivesMatter to Black Liberation.* Haymarket Books.

Verhaeghe, P. (1998). *Love in the Time of Loneliness: Three Essays on Drive and Desire.* Karnac Books.

Weil, S. (1955). *Oppression and Liberty* (A. Wills & J. Petrie, Trans.). Routledge; *Oppression et liberté,* Éditions Gallimard.

Žižek, S. (1986). *Pathological Narcissus as a Socially Mandatory Form of Subjectivity.* (Narcisistička kultura, Naprijed, Zagreb, 1986). Translation on: http://www.manifesta.org/manifesta3/catalogue5.htm

CHAPTER 4

The Crisis of Initiation

Abstract This chapter argues that a crisis of initiation marks our age, and it looks at the concept of initiation more broadly from a psychoanalytic perspective. It then analyzes the Oedipal process and how it was situated in the period prior to neoliberalism.

Keywords Initiation • Oedipus • Adulthood • Frankfurt School • Slovene Lacanian theorists • Lacan • Name-of-the-Father

Perhaps the most far-ranging damage the rise of the social superego inflicts on psychic life is how it distorts stages of self-making and becoming. The rampant marketization of everyday life results in a subjective crisis, witnessed by an increasing sense that the very experience of adulthood is stunted, that we have a delayed adolescence and a rising infantilization of social life. According to many widely accepted institutional metrics of business and civil society organizations today, one remains a "youth" up to 30 or even 35 years of age.[1]

---

[1] For a provocative reading of the "death of adulthood" in American culture, see A.O. Scott's article "The Death of Adulthood in American Culture," *New York Times*, 2014 https://www.nytimes.com/2014/09/14/magazine/the-death-of-adulthood-in-american-culture.html

© The Author(s), under exclusive license to Springer Nature Switzerland AG 2022
D. Tutt, *Psychoanalysis and the Politics of the Family: The Crisis of Initiation*, The Palgrave Lacan Series,
https://doi.org/10.1007/978-3-030-94070-6_4

In this chapter we argue this crisis is centered around a wider crisis of initiation, that is, a crisis around identifications and rituals that initiate the subject into new stages of self-development and maturity. The crisis over adulthood points to a far-wider crisis over communal belonging, friendship, and ties with others. By "initiation," we don't mean an esoteric induction into a secret society or a religious rite or ritual. However, the term has these important legacies attached to it, which should be studied and taken seriously.[2] Instead, by a crisis of initiation, we seek to name a historical backdrop concept for understanding how the hyper-marketization of the neoliberal period affects our psychic, social, and interpersonal ties.

How is the family tied up with the crisis of initiation? As we saw in our chapter "The Family Spirit and Social Reproduction," the family is tasked with regulating a series of rites that establish it as "a united and integrated entity" that is "stable, constant, and indifferent to the fluctuations of individual feelings" (Bourdieu, 1998, p. 198). What rites produce are shared affects; they create a singular "family feeling"— that is, rites enable the family to function as what Bourdieu calls a "field" where physical, symbolic, and economic power relations are linked to the volume and structure of the capital possessed by each member. The struggle of the family centers on the maintenance of these power relations.

The family is a system where these secular rites—these are not religious rites, after all—ensure the perpetuation of a family spirit that neutralizes the illusion of separateness and gives the family a singular identity. This is a process that the state has carefully cultivated, but these family rites are undergoing a crisis of initiation. According to Bourdieu, the family spirit consists of "the absorption of disappointment, the establishment of expectations, the charting of the way for a life of stability, or not" (p. 107). Therefore, those without family do not have this interior pact. We can discuss working-class families who have often split apart and been thrown into horizontal care networks and deprived of the family spirit. But despite this deprivation, those subjects without family spirit often find ways to

---

[2] It is worth considering, and future research should be done on the esoteric dimension of initiation and far-right and neofascist politics today. In the traditionalist René Guénon and Julias Evola, a major onus is placed on initiatory community, esotericism, and the importance of the secret mystical group. This even led these thinkers to consider Marxism as a form of "counter-initiation" which makes for an interesting insight, especially given the way we raise the concept of counter-initiation in this work. See the chapter "The Political Stakes of the Social Superego."

muster a different sort of abundance, and they point to a future of a revolutionary conception of the family.

We are once again confronted with a similar paradox to the paradox of liberation: the waning of the efficacy of the family spirit opens a potential source of emancipation; that is, it seems as if the family is freed from the same Oedipal superegoic mechanism it formerly had. But we must be cautious before simply stating that the social superego is a maternal replacement function in the wake of Oedipus. In his later work, Lasch adopted an essentially conservative reactionary position to the dynamics of the social superego by advocating the strengthening of the family in such a way that he derided the left for many of its family abolition positions.[3]

From a Laschian perspective, the delay of adulthood can be read as caused by the inefficacy of ego ideals caused by the family no longer having autonomy, or a breathing room, from marketization. As the feminist writer and critic of Lasch, Jessica Benjamin (1988) has argued, implicit in Lasch's theory of the culture of narcissism is the idealization of the father as a liberator (p. 233). Thus, while for Lasch, Narcissus has replaced Oedipus as the myth of our time, the Oedipus complex remains the preferred, if not inevitable, solution for resolving this crisis of initiation and developing more autonomous, rational individuals.

Against the argument of Michéa and Lasch, we argue that the rise of the social superego intensifies the figures of both the mother and the father, displacing them as impassable imaginary barriers that are transposed onto authority relations. In these conditions, the figure of the father can take on, at least psychically, at least a feeling of total omnipotence and or castration. Such a condition only leads to a culture that cannot manage social conflict adequately, wherein cancellation of the other and hyper-purification of other opinions or lifestyles and so on must be done away with entirely. The paradox that emerges here, and psychoanalysis instructs us in this paradox, is that the imaginary father cannot be killed. The imaginary father is Oedipus at Colonus; blinded, already dead symbolically, his injunctions are dead weight. In the context of our time, the father's absence—as this more general socialized form of authority/otherness—is felt even more intensely.

---

[3] To get a better idea of Lasch's critique of the way the New Left and psychoanalytic Marxists such as Herbert Marcuse and Norman O. Brown were fusing Freud and Marx, see his essay "The Freudian Left and the Cultural Revolution," September/October 1981.

Consider our contemporary dynamic of crisis in paternal authority relations to what Adorno and Horkheimer (1975) saw in the early bourgeois model of the father and authority:

> Under the pressure of the father children were supposed to learn not to conceive failures in terms of their societal causation, but to stop at the individual aspect and to render this absolute in terms of guilt, inadequacy and personal inferiority. If this pressure was not too harsh, and above all, if it was softened by maternal tenderness, then this resulted in human beings who were also capable of seeing faults in themselves; human beings who learned through the father's example an attitude of independence, a joy in free dispositions and inner discipline; who could represent authority as well as freedom and could practice these. Where the family was adequate to its tasks, they gained a conscience, a capacity to love, and consistency. This was productive and progressive. (p. 141)

This baseline initiatory structure of the Oedipal dynamic afforded a certain room and space for the subject to treat the wider field of otherness so that it was more likely the subject could work through imaginary aggressions and transcend those attachments and identifications. There is thus certain rationalism at the heart of the Oedipal dynamic where power, conflict, and antagonisms are managed with greater resolve and sense. This reading of Oedipus we are proposing must remain cautious: we are not aiming to sneak a patriarchal family structure and social order in through the backdoor. We propose that, in addition to the structuring feature of the social superego, the crisis of the social order must also be understood as stemming from a certain deformation of Oedipus, not a total absence. We are not post-Oedipal. Just as we have proposed that the rise of the social superego has been brought on by the expansion of liberatory demands realized through hyper-marketization, these same forces have disrupted the basis of Oedipal dynamics. These are dynamics, lest we forget, which aim to transcend psychic fixations on paternal authority relations.

Oedipus is a theory for the *working-through* of paternal dependencies; it is a theory aimed at a more thorough liberation of desire. Lacan's theory of Oedipus, although he would not use this term "Oedipus" provides the tools for re-thinking this problematic because it aims to address the lingering patriarchal residue of Oedipus by de-mythologizing the theory and looking at it as a *function* of desire and, ultimately, of the freedom of desire. Despite all its baggage and bad reputation, we retain this term because it is a familiar term. Moreover, the way we invoke this term is not to be understood as clinical or even individualist. But instead, we mean Oedipus as a more general form of subjective change.

The proposal that contemporary capitalism creates conditions of a "delayed Oedipus" or even a "reversal of Oedipus" is already widely accepted by several psychoanalytic thinkers.[4] Furthermore, the periodization we are working with—the 1970s to the present—is marked by a stunting of adulthood. However, the forces that contribute to the delay of adulthood have been observed long before this period. For example, in Adorno and other Frankfurt School theorists of the rise of the Culture Industry after World War II, the "cult of the adolescent body" is a feature of the rise of the Culture Industry in the early-to-mid-twentieth century. Larry Rickels (2002) has examined how fetishization of adolescence functions as a collective defense mechanism against mourning of mass death which permits psychopathic violence. Rickels ties this process to Nazi Germany before the outbreak of World War II.[5]

The Slovene Lacanian School argues that the Freudian Oedipal function is not a theory of subjective normativity; that is, it is not a function reducible to a patriarchal social order, nor is it a biological theory. In the work of Slavoj Žižek, Mladen Dolar, and Alenka Zupančič, Oedipus is recast in a Lacanian theoretical formulation and re-thought as a mechanism that does not reinforce a conservative symbolic. They argue for an interpretation of Oedipus as a theory of *psychic disequilibrium* that plays a pivotal role, not in adjusting to a given social order, but Oedipus marks a break with the dominant social order. Oedipus is a psychic maladjustment to ego ideals of a social order. This view is a powerful corrective to the more widely held account of Oedipus as Deleuze and Guattari theorized,

---

[4] This theme is explored in the following chapters and there is a wide swath of contemporary Lacanian theorists, including Dany Robert Darfour, Jacques Alain Miller, and Alain Badiou, who each theorize our epoch as marked by a "stunting of Oedipus." This is after all a key insight of Lacan himself, and it should be noted that Lacan did not use the term "Oedipus complex" but paternal function. This is not to say that Lacan rejects or abandons the more fundamental insights that surround the Oedipus complex and for that reason we also retain the term.

[5] In *Nazi Psychoanalysis* Vols. I and II Laurence Rickels discusses how the Nazis fetishization of adolescence and of the adolescent body was deployed to normalize a society of continuous psychopathic violence. Rickels: "There is a society wide tendency of unmournable death, which is a major reason why the cult of the adolescent body is created, to fend off this impossible proximity to death. In the adolescent terminal, transference doesn't stop."

namely that Oedipal logics are a Kantian a priori which was not furnished by psychoanalysis but by the structuring effects of capitalist life; that is, it is the social structuring effects of capitalism that Oedipalizes, not an idealist psychic process. In the Slovene interpretation, Oedipus is not an idealist reflection of a given social order but a mode of subjective singularity. Oedipus is a theory of initiation that is an essential feature in understanding subjective emancipation.

References

A.O. Scott. (2014). The Death of Adulthood in American Culture. *New York Times*. See: https://www.nytimes.com/2014/09/14/magazine/the-death-of-adulthood-in-american-culture.html

Adorno, T., & Horkheimer, M. (1975). *"The Family" Critical Theory Selected Essays*. Continuum.

Benjamin, J. (1988). *Bonds of Love: Psychoanalysis, Feminism and the Problem of Domination*. Random House.

Bourdieu, P. (1998). *Practical Reason*. Stanford University Press.

Lasch, C. (1981). The Freudian Left and the Cultural Revolution. *New Left Review, 129*, 23–34.

Rickels, L. (2002). *Nazi Psychoanalysis Vol. I: Only Psychoanalysis Won the War*. University of Minnesota Press.

CHAPTER 5

Oedipus: A Function of Initiation

Abstract This chapter examines Lacan's theory of the Name-of-the-Father and his revision of the Freudian Oedipus complex, and argues that the concept of initiation remains a crucial way of understanding the Oedipal function. We then turn to a historical examination of the crisis of initiation of the contemporary period by looking at Lacan's theory of the discourses, specifically the effects of the fifth "capitalist" discourse and its propensity to erode social bonds. We examine how the initiation crisis concerned Lacan in his later years and how it affects subjectivity today.

Keywords Capitalist discourse • Crisis of initiation • Initiation • Lacan • Name-of-the-Father • Fort/da game

In an early essay titled "Family Complexes in the Formation of the Individual" (1938), Lacan discusses the origin of the family and how the Freudian notion of the "complex" emerges concerning the family. Lacan demonstrates that cultural factors condition a complex at the expense of natural instincts, by which he suggests that the family objectifies mental identifications, not instincts. We can understand this distinction between mental identifications and instincts in the example of jealousy. Lacan argues that the jealous rivalry between siblings "can still manifest itself long after the subject has been weaned and is no longer in a situation of

© The Author(s), under exclusive license to Springer Nature Switzerland AG 2022
D. Tutt, *Psychoanalysis and the Politics of the Family: The Crisis of Initiation*, The Palgrave Lacan Series,
https://doi.org/10.1007/978-3-030-94070-6_5

vital competition with his brother." In the heat of sibling rivalry, jealousy is libidinally charged beyond merely an identification mechanism. Over time, like the jealousy of sibling rivalry fades in intensity, there remains what Lacan calls a "passive identification" that lingers on even after the siblings have overcome their jealous rivalries.

This trace of mental identification marks familial conflicts, and it is why even long after a family rivalry, dispute, or argument formally ends, it is often hard to feel as if it has truly ended, as the passive form of the identification lives on. These *passive mental identifications* revolve around the idea of a "complex," or a conditioning structure that the family develops. In this early essay, Lacan (1938) stresses that a combination of cultural factors drives the family complexes at the expense of natural or biological factors. Family complexes thus not only are conditioned by the cultural and social context, but also produce distinct objects of reference, what Lacan calls "an unconscious representation known as the imago" (p. 24).

Imagos are both biological—rooted in instinct and libido—and material, that is, rooted in social and cultural relations. Importantly, imagos must be sublimated to introduce new relationships with the social group, and new complexes can be integrated into the psyche. In the case of the imago of the mother, it is in weaning from breastfeeding that the child learns to sublimate the imago of the mother, which has its place deep in the psyche. Still, this process, like the experience of jealousy in sibling rivalry, enters a more passive stage—the child pulls at the mother's apron strings and latches onto the mother for years after weaning ends. If this sublimation of the imago of the mother, in this case of breastfeeding, is stunted or resisted by the child, the very progress of the child's personality is affected. This stunted sublimation of imagos was a widely experienced psychic phenomenon and it made the basis of neurosis and the experience of neurotics during the period in which Freud wrote and in which psychoanalysis was coming to fruition.

We raise these important dynamics that combine social/cultural and biological/libidinal dynamics that make up family complexes to note that the social fabric of the family conditions family complexes. This insight means social and cultural dynamics are central over any biological basis of analysis, which means that the family is not a transhistorical structure. That the Oedipus complex was the "great neurosis" of Freud's time was a sign of the early decline of the Oedipus complex itself. As Lacan remarks, "the personality of the father, which is always lacking in some way or another, whether he be absent or humiliated, divided or a sham. It is this lack which, as explained by our theory of the Oedipus complex, exhausts instinctual energy and vitiates the dialectic of sublimation" (p. 114). The social crisis at the origin of psychoanalysis during the late nineteenth century and early twentieth century affected the imago of the father. It is this crisis that created the pre-conditions for the Oedipus complex. As Lacan (1938) writes:

> The role of the imago of the father allows itself to be glimpsed in a striking way in the formation of most great men ... But a large number of psychological effects seem to us to be a function of the social decline of the paternal imago. A decline conditioned by the recurrence in the individual of the extreme effects of social progress, a decline that marks itself above all these days in the collectivities most marked by these effects: economic concentration, political catastrophes. Such that the future will follow, this decline constitutes a psychological crisis. Possibly it is with this crisis that it is necessary to relate the appearance of psychoanalysis itself. (p 112)

Neuroses are formed based on family complexes, and these complexes are structured by the social conditions of the given time. In Freud's time, the Oedipus complex was the dominant form of the family complex. This is why it is crucial to keep in mind the social context in which Lacan will propose a revision to the structure of the Oedipus complex in the 1950s through the entirety of his teachings up to the late 1970s. This is a period in time that marks a break from the Freudian period. Indeed, Lacan proposes a profound revision to the Freudian Oedipus complex in what he coined as the "Name-of-the-Father," wherein he meant to work through this problem of the historical mutations to (and of) the Oedipus complex in social life. For Lacan, the Oedipus complex refers to a type of identification by which the subject transcends the aggressiveness that is constitutive of their first subjective individuation (pp. 95 and 117). In the Oedipus complex, the subject creates an ego ideal based on the image of the father. About the ego ideal, Lacan (1938) writes:

> But what interests me here is what I shall refer to as the "pacifying" function of the ego-ideal: the connection between its libidinal normativeness and a cultural normativeness, bound up since the dawn of history with the imago of the father. (p. 175)

In Lacan's revision of the Freudian Oedipus complex, he scraps the term "complex" for "paternal function." For Lacan, the father is not a biological function, but a function bound up with language and desire. Lacan identifies three moments of the Oedipal identification in the child's early life. The first moment is best expressed in the example that Freud gives of his grandson's "fort/da" game. In this game, the child plays with a toy that is bound by a string. He throws the toy away from his crib, expressing a "fort!" (away), and then pulls the toy back toward him with a "da!" (there). This movement of play represents an attempt to come to terms with staging the absence and presence of the mother.

The fort/da game, according to Lacan, is centered around the creation of a lack. It portrays the moment the child is born into language. The object the child makes appear and disappear is less important for Lacan (2006) than the phonemic distinction of the fort and da; it is this distinction that is "the point of insemination for a symbolic order that preexists the infantile subject and in accordance with which he has to structure himself" (496). When the child says "fort/da" the child disappears in being—it is nothing and emerges *as subject*—namely, as an effect of language and can now act as a subject by mobilizing his desire as a desire of a subject toward objects that substitute for the lost object. The game is thus ultimately about symbolic mastery of a lost object, the maternal desire, and the process of the child's access to the symbolic register, or the order of language and speech.

The fort/da game is an accessible example of how the subject moves from the imaginary to the symbolic. In this movement, desire is experienced as what Lacan famously calls the "desire of the Other." The child develops autonomy in this first stage through identification with the law of the mother, but this law can only be accessed by recourse to the father's function. That function is precisely to metaphorize the mother's desire. "The Oedipal identification," says Lacan (2006), "is that by which the subject transcends the aggressivity that is constitutive of the primary subjective individuation" (p. 23). The first moment of Oedipus thus represents the superego laying down its authority in the register of the imaginary, which is often the voice of the father, and Freud says the superego is independent from the conscious ego but intimate with the unconscious id.

A second key point that Lacan makes in *Seminar V, The Formations of the Unconscious* (1957–1958), is that the father in the Oedipus complex is a metaphor; that is, the signifier of the father comes in place of another signifier. Because the first signifier introduced into symbolization is the maternal signifier. This we saw in the example of the fort-da game, the father substitutes this signifier in the form of S in place of S. The paternal metaphor that the father stands in for is, in fact, only a substitution of the father qua symbol, qua signifier in place of the mother" (2017), which is why the signifier of the father ensures that the phallus remains in the imaginary plane.

The father is the symbolic figure mediating the unknown desire beyond the child's relation to the maternal desire. To give the subject access to the "beyond" of the mother's desire, the signifier of the father is the nodal point in the Oedipus complex, and the subject is put into an existential crisis: to be or not to be this phallus? Now that we have provided a background in how the Oedipal identification process works, we want to consider how this process becomes re-inscribed onto other objects, and ask to what extent the Oedipus complex creates a "daddy-mommy-me" complex. Our argument hinges on this idea that the stunting of Oedipal dynamics is not merely reducible to the family itself, but that it is a complex that is transposed onto institutional life from schools to the workplace. Oedipus proliferates outward from the subject to the social. This is what concerned Deleuze and Guattari in their critique of Oedipus, which we will examine below. However, as the Lacanian psychoanalyst Raul Moncayo (2012) points out, "Oedipal desire is mobilized against the lack in the other rather than against the repressive strength of the Other" (pp. 104–106). This means that Oedipal subjectivity concerns the autonomous realization of desire. Therefore, Oedipus should and can be thought of as emancipation that provides the conditions of new relations of desire and new openings of desire.

In *Seminar XVIII, On a Discourse That Might Not Be a Semblant* (1971), Lacan remarks:

> The myth of the Oedipus complex causes trouble in some way, is that not so, because supposedly it establishes the primacy of the Father, which is supposed to be a kind of reflection of patriarchy. I would like to make you sense something which, through which, for me at least, it appears to me to be not at all a patriarchal reflection. Far from it. "It shows us simply this: a point first of all through which castration might be circumscribed, through a logical approach and, in the way that I will designate as being numeral." (p. 12)

What is at stake in the Oedipus complex is the instantiation of a point through symbolic castration. Castration establishes a point that situates the subject in a different relation to the maternal; that is, the function of castration is numerical: it establishes a zero. The father has a starting point, and the mother does not.

To recall our breakdown of the Oedipal moments, the crucial moment in the Oedipal drama is the third movement, where an impasse over desire occurs, wherein the subject undergoes a stunting and a hampering of their desire. This state of subjective crisis is akin to living in the time of Hamlet, that is, living in the father's time and unable to break free from it. The third and final movement is a movement of resolution, a movement of *initiation* of the son or daughter. A resolution to this movement importantly does require the intervention if a father but importantly, this does not have to be the biological or even the primary father figure. The father function here, Lacan notes, is contingent and "plural": the "Names"—and not merely the Name—of the father are stressed here.

Lacan argues the father (figure) intervenes not by prohibiting the desire but by *permitting* the desire of the subject. This shift from a prohibitory intervention to a permissive intervention—the father enacts a "Yes" to the subject's desire, an affirmation that resolves the impasse of the subject's desire. This emphasis on permissiveness is a crucial insight Lacan offers and it differs from the Freudian theory of a prohibitionary father, and it is an insight that is historically specific to our epoch. What is the function of the "yes" at this stage? Its message is the following: you may form a new *jouissance* or enjoyment, and this is what enables the son/daughter to break from the impasse that Oedipus introduces from the very beginning, in stage two (Lacan, 2006, p. 321).

We have here a saga of psychic autonomy, a story of a series of movements that steadily *break apart the reliance of the subject on paternal authority and pressures*. But, for Lacan, the Oedipus complex has a degree of *ruin* and destruction at stake in its movements, and this ruin is of the imaginary itself. As Lacan (1993) remarks, "the Oedipus complex means that the imaginary, in itself is an incestuous and conflictual relation, is doomed to conflict and ruin" (p. 96).

As pointed out in *Seminar V, Formations of the Unconscious*, Lacan (2017) describes his revision of the Oedipus complex by pointing out the counterintuitive point that Oedipus never becomes a subject because as a being, he is *deprived of becoming a subject*; that is, Oedipus is a story of a *failed initiation*. In this way, a decline of Oedipus such as we experience today is also a further intensification of Oedipus. We track and develop how this intensification of Oedipus affects our politics and psychic relations to authority in Chaps. 8 and 9. The decline of this basic initiatory procedure has to do with a stunting in achieving independent desire.

As Alenka Zupančič argues (2000), the Oedipus tragedy has to do with the consequences of entry into the symbolic, "Oedipus is the tragedy of entry into the symbolic itself" (p. 191). The tragedy occurs when Oedipus claims that he is not even capable of being guilty. In other words, Oedipus was deprived of his very destiny as a subject of desire upon entry into the symbolic. Furthermore, it is essential to note that Oedipus did not kill his father because he did not have a symbolic father. Rather, Oedipus kills the fact that the father cannot live up to the father's function, and this makes the insult that Oedipus suffers revolve around the fact that he is not permitted to be guilty. Thus, Oedipus is the *objet petit a*, which Žižek defines as "the paradoxical object generated by language itself as the material leftover of the purely self-referential movement of signifiers" (p. 194).

The entire point of the Oedipus myth, in this reading, shifts from one about proper adjustment to a symbolic, or Oedipus as a normalizing function, to a situation where the subject is radically estranged from the symbolic as such.[1] In this innovative Lacanian re-reading of the Oedipus myth, we are presented with a story about how the subject is born into a symbolic that has failed. This failure is the very core of the Oedipal process for all subjects. Unlike Hamlet, who refuses castration, Oedipus undergoes castration and affirms a new time—Oedipus attains something singular. In contrast, Hamlet persists in the world without undergoing castration, which is why "time is out of joint" for Hamlet. Hamlet is thrust into the time of his father and cannot escape it; he must bring it to a conclusion so his own time can start. But he is judged guilty at the level of his being, at the level of his very existence, whereas for Oedipus, his guilt is foreclosed as he is not permitted to live in the time of the father because he is deprived of the father's symbolic entirely. The Oedipal break is a metaphor of psychic disruption within the social field and the symbolic. It is a story of how through the antagonism with the family itself the subject works through and overcomes psychic attachments and impediments to come to exist in a more singular and liberated way.

But what does the crisis of Oedipus have to do with the concept of initiation? As we have laid out, the crisis of initiation is a constitutive moment of the Oedipal process that revolves around the following argument: the father must validate the child/subject to develop a sense of movement out of the desire of the mother. This "father" does not have to be thought of as a traditional father figure or even as a patriarchal father figure, i.e., stand-in father figures are necessary for initiating the third moment in the drama of Oedipus. This remains an important point to keep centered and one that the socialist-feminist tradition has acknowledged and at other times completely refused.

---

[1] To quote Zupančič (2000): "It [Oedipus] situates the source of tragedy in fully, 'one hundred percent completely' accomplished symbolization in the word, after the appearance of which the Sphinx vanishes without trace. What 'seals the fate' of Oedipus is not some hidden remainder of the Sphinx/Thing, but precisely the word and its consequences (its remainder). Hence Oedipus' ruin will be brought about by the fact that he will remain (albeit involuntarily) true to his word."

In other words, there is a tendency to claim, as we will see in our critique of Deleuze and Guattari's *Anti-Oedipus*, that the entirety of the Freudian theory of Oedipus only reinforces a patriarchal and father-dominated household and mode of authority. We believe that the insights of Lacan, especially in his later work, moves beyond this inevitability. What Lacan's revision of the Oedipus complex offers is an insight into the contemporary family. In the very concept of the Names-of-the-Father, we have a theory of how the impasse of desire, of frustrated and stunted subjectivity is a common experience and psychic affliction that we face today. From this insight, we can begin to understand Oedipus as a tool the subject uses to cross the intrinsic problem of jouissance[2] and resolve this impasse.

The Names-of-the-Father is a pragmatic instrument that can be used toward the service of goods it initiates, typically through identification with a father, wherein one is faced with the fact that *one always chooses a father*. The decline of Oedipus in our present society is less a decline than it is an intensification of the malfunction of this tool, a stunting, and hay-wiring, a glitch in the Oedipal movements. It is not a matter of "choosing" a father, although that is common for the plural stage three dynamic. Also, it should be noted that one often does not even know that the process of identification with an effective father stand-in is taking place. The Oedipal drama is often only realized far after the work has been done, so to speak. Think here of the mentor in a workplace, an older musician for the younger aspiring person, or an often unsuspecting and random presence in one's life that functionally brings about a cessation and positive mutation to the Oedipal drama. Like any complex, it is not an easy cure or fix. As Freud once confided to Ernest Jones, there remains an element of the Oedipus complex that cannot be fully cured or transcended.

We have argued that the first historical period of Oedipus that Freud inaugurates coincides with the birth of the bourgeois family in the nineteenth and turn of the twentieth century. A shift then occurs in the structure of the family that is only intensified from the 1970s onward. As we examined in Chap. 2, these changes have overwhelmed the family and given rise to a socialization of the superego driven by hyper-marketization resulting in the loss and increasing difficulty for the family to mediate subjective life. In Lacan's later work, starting in the late 1970's up to his

---

[2] We do not analyze the important concept of jouissance in this book, but we do suggest that readers consider a more careful elaboration of the concept in Lacan's teaching by considering Jacques-Alain Miller's work "Six Paradigms of Jouissance" (Miller, 2019).

death in 1981, he repeatedly discusses these changes and the capitalist dynamics propelling them. To get at the heart of the initiation crisis, we thus need to understand Lacan's wider theory of the discourses he presents in his most political of seminars, *The Other Side of Psychoanalysis, Seminar XVII*, delivered in 1968. Lacan proposes four interrelated discourses that each produce a distinct "social link."

The theory of the discourses points to the proposal that enjoyment is produced via a discourse: an account for how different configurations of power and subjective agency forge distinct social links and bonds. The originary discourse of the four is what Lacan calls the "master's discourse," which forms a solution to the social bond by establishing a law that determines some as masters. In conversation with the philosopher and diplomat Alexandre Kojève's teachings on Hegel's master-slave dialectic, Lacan will propose that the master's discourse produces a law, or "master signifier" that is put to work by a divided subject.[3] The injunctions of the master's law take the form of speech and commands that Lacan represents as a "matheme" symbol of "S1." When the master's speech enters discourse, it challenges the knowledge or "S2" one has about oneself, thus creating the dimension of the divided subject or "$." The divided subject is divided between the signifier of the master's discourse and the body they put to work to fulfill the master's demand, and the labor of the divided subject creates a surplus of enjoyment, a remainder that Lacan represents under the sign "a."

The master's discourse is not a closed repetition of this division process, but it does possess a certain efficacy in the fact that it puts the master's signifiers or S1 to work. A social order structured around the master's discourse is one in which the placement of the S1 is not under dispute: the master signifiers determine the castration of the subject. This castration is based on a sacrifice of the body put to work by the slave or divided subject based on the master's injunctions and commands. The first rupture in the discourse of the master emerges when the slave poses a question as to the legitimacy of the master's speech. When the subject's division is *elevated as a symptom*, the hysteric's discourse emerges (Lacan, 2007, pp. 30–34).

The hysteric discourse reverses the position of knowledge from repetitively putting to work the S1 of the master to making the division. This process produces the matter of knowledge. The hysteric is thus the first

---

[3] We already saw the basis of Lacan's theory of the "divided subject" in the example of the fort/da game.

figure to name the symptom and to *pose their symptom as a matter of truth*. The hysteric brings out the knowledge of their division to the agent of power S1, producing a new knowledge about their condition that generates a new surplus enjoyment for the subject.

The hysteric produces a new knowledge S2 of the master's discourse and occupies the position of *a* or the truth of the master's discourse in her act of defiance. However, the hysteric does not give up her knowledge of the symptom, and in this persistence, she unmasks the master's function. Although historically, Lacan will suggest the hysteric's discourse is found in the figure of Socrates' teachings which insist on a fundamental unknowability of the master's knowledge, in Socrates' case, it was the false and inadequate knowledge of the Sophist's knowledge of the state.

The university discourse emerges historically under the reign of Charlemagne,[4] and its dynamic is one in which the subject seeks knowledge S2 by addressing a question of its own subjective singularity S1 to the field of knowledge a. In this movement, the subject is delivered to knowledge but deprived of its capacity to resolve their singularity and thus remains divided $. The problem with the university discourse is that the subject re-circulates knowledge in service to a wider field of knowledge, but *it does not produce distinction S1 for itself.* Lacan discusses how "making a name for yourself" becomes elevated to an empty gesture in the university discourse and that the situation produces a profound emptiness and shame.

Freud historically founds the fourth discourse or the analyst's discourse. It is based on the analysand coming to analysis with a knowledge of their subjective division and suffering $. They address an analyst who possesses a certain knowledge that the discourse is founded on a non-relation; that is, the analyst listens for the symptoms of the divided subject and through the analytic process works-through developing a new knowledge of the analysand's symptom, thus producing a new S1. We can see now that we have come full circle from the master's discourse that starts with the master-signifier in the position of agency to the analyst's discourse which now produces a new knowledge S1 from the working-through of the symptom of the analysand. Lacan (1971) summarizes the four discourses

---

[4] It is interesting to note that each of the four discourses also has a historical figure that marks their beginning: that represent the beginning of each discourse: Lycurgus the Spartan military ruler for the Master's, Charlemagne for the University, Socrates for the Hysteric, and Freud for the Analyst; see Lacan, 1970.

in the following way in *Seminar XVIII, On a Discourse That Might Not Be Semblant*:

> It is when the master signifier is at a certain place that I speak about the discourse of the Master; when a certain knowledge also occupies it, I speak of that of the University; when the subject in its division, fundamental for the unconscious, is in place there, I speak about the discourse of the Hysteric, and finally when surplus enjoying occupies it, I speak about the discourse of the Analyst. (pp. 38–39)

The fifth discourse, what Lacan calls the "capitalist discourse," concerns our wider investigation of the initiation crisis. In 1972, Lacan delivered a lecture titled the "Milan Discourse" (1972), where he elaborates on the capitalist discourse by first starting with defining what a discourse is: "What is a discourse? It is what, in the order … in the ordering of what can be produced by the existence of language, makes some social link function" (p. 1). The capitalist discourse is markedly different from the other four because it does not produce a social link. This absence correlates to a crisis of subjective initiation.

Like the university discourse, the S1 or master-signifier is a bi-product of the market in the capitalist discourse. It is not derived through a symbolically castrating process with an other. As Stijn Vanheule (2016) has brilliantly summarized, the capitalist discourse starts with a divided subject $ who addresses the market S1 for a solution to their division. The market provides a solution in the form of a commodity S2 which produces a surplus enjoyment but forecloses the question of the subject's division and desire. This foreclosure of the subject's division means that capitalism puts off the question of castration and instead only re-circulates surplus enjoyment back onto the divided subject $ like a game of roulette. In the other discourses, the preservation of lack creates space for contestations and challenges mastery, whereas the capitalist discourse follows a different logic. In the other discourses, castration instantiates points of initiatory movement, but in the capitalist discourse, no such points are firmly established.

As Todd McGowan (2016) has suggested, the capitalist discourse takes desire *as if* it was a frustrated demand and translates desire into pragmatic solutions, thus treating desire as a demand that should be gratified (pp. 24–25). Lacan writes, "[t]he crisis we face is since the capitalist discourse turns only on itself; there is no movement possible from it to any of the other discourses and the movement internal to the capitalist discourse is fundamentally different from that in the other discourses" (Klein, p. 4). The capitalist discourse possesses an infinite number of ways to deal with subjective division through the market and its clever development of more and more commodities to satisfy desire, which is why Lacan argues the capitalist discourse exploits desire by treating it as a specific question to be answered by means of practical solutions (Vanheule, 2016). Therefore, Lacan's theory of the capitalist discourse should be read not as a literal condition facing subjectivity but as a tendency that is affecting subjectivity.

The capitalist discourse is less of a theory than a profound insight,[5] and several social and cultural phenomena can be drawn out from the theory of the discourses. The first important point, apropos our argument that the capitalist discourse accelerates a crisis of subjective initiation is that we have experienced in the post-1970s period an intensification and re-birth of religion and religious practice around the world. It is also noteworthy here that the crisis of initiation that Lacan points to additionally concerns the status of belief because the subject relates to the symbolic order with a different form of disavowal and cynicism. Lacan even refers to our age and epoch as the age of the "*les non-dupes errant*"—an insight he draws from the wider crisis of initiation, which for Lacan is primarily bound up with the fact that there is no sexual relation.

In his classical humor and wit, Lacan will make a homophony between "le nom du pere" (Name-of-the-Father) and "les non dupes errent" (the non-duped error), which he entitled a year of his teachings in 1973. The homophony at play here references the seminar Lacan never delivered on the Name-of-the-Father in 1963 course that became the "Non-Existent Seminar" as Lacan faced expulsion from the International Psychoanalytic Institute (IPA) the same year. The title of *Seminar XXII, The Non-Duped Err*, hints at the broader social dynamics of the decline of the Oedipus myth as a mode of subjective life, and Lacan begins the seminar with a set of reflections on the crisis of initiation. In this seminar, Lacan has identified a new cynicism in the wider culture based on a certain common knowledge of the non-existent sexual relation. Lacan remarks that today,

---

[5] Given that the theory of the discourses is in many ways seriously altered and modified in Lacan's development of the "Borromean clinic" in his later years, it is fair to suggest that the theory of the discourses, as the psychoanalyst Gabriel Tupinambá has said, are "not a theory but a schema for organizing disparate insights on heterogeneous matters" (private correspondence).

people know "there is nothing behind the real except what one must hold onto." Those who refuse to be duped by this common knowledge, who take the collapse of symbolic efficiency literally, suffer.

This crisis of initiation and the new cynicism calls for a new ethics founded on the refusal of being "unduped" by this new symbolic fiction. The pragmatic solutions offered up by the capitalist discourse pose a problem for the subject's capacity to handle the problem of enjoyment itself. Lacan will define initiation as a "science of enjoyment," that is, a particular organization of enjoyment configured and produced in the four discourses. But in the capitalist discourse, the superego's demand to enjoy only offers more enjoyment. The capitalist discourse thus leaves subjects with nothing but unresolvable enjoyment riddled by the emptiness of their condition:

> Initiation presents itself, when one looks at the thing closely, always as this: an approach, an approach that does not happen without all sorts of detours, of deliberation, an approach of something where what is opened, revealed, is something which strictly concerns enjoyment. I mean that it is not unthinkable that the body, the body in so far as we believe it to be living, is something that is much more clever than what the anatomical physiologists know. There is perhaps a science of enjoyment, if one can express it thus. Initiation in any case cannot be defined otherwise. There is only one misfortune, which is that in our day, *there is no longer a trace, absolutely anywhere of initiation.* (Lacan, 1971, 57)

The crisis of initiation has been expressed and theorized in the school of Jacques-Alain Miller, one of the great translators and interpreters of Lacan. Miller has argued, at least since the mid-1990s onward, that society is no longer organized around a master signifier, an S1, but that our compass or the "dominant place" in our civilization is that of the *objet petit a*. Taking up Lacan's suggestions in *Seminar XX, "Encore"* (1972–1973)—and elsewhere—that industrially produced surplus jouissance, *"plus-de-jouir"* produces, "a completely different imperative – *Jouis.*" Moreover, Miller argues that this *jouis* forms a demand to enjoy that is the superego of our civilization.

In our time, Miller and Laurent (1998) write, "it is both men and women who are defined by their isolation in jouissance. Their withdrawal there is the rise of object a to the zenith of the social" (p. 30). Miller has named this crisis at the heart of our civilizational conjecture "the Other no longer exists." In his presentation to his psychoanalytic school, the World Association of Psychoanalysis at Commandatuba, Brazil, in 2005, Miller says the "plus-de jouir" acts on disoriented subjects, producing an S1 that is taken up superegoically as a form of incessant subjective evaluation. The Millerian Lacanian analyst and theorist Thomas Svolos (2017) points out that this superego pressure can be seen in the explosion of signifiers we find in social media: the constant evaluation of one's own tweets and Facebook wall postings, of every aspect and thought and impulse of our lives. In this situation, knowledge, S2, is in the position of the hidden truth (or lie); knowledge now is nothing but a semblant (p. 87). In this Millerian description of the contemporary world, psychoanalysis is granted a unique role in assigning master signifiers by way of the analyst's discourse. But, as Lacan continually argued from the early 1970s to his death, the capitalist discourse poses a grave threat to the very existence of psychoanalysis as an institution. It is important to recognize, however, that Miller's political position amidst is contradictory; he is acutely aware of this crisis but he has lent his support to neoliberal political parties and to a renewed political commitment to preserving the liberal status quo (Tupinambá, pp. 15–17).[6]

Why have we chosen the concept of a crisis of initiation to describe the wider problems with the family and the politics that surround subjectivity today? In his study of initiation rites, the psychoanalyst Bruno Bettelheim identifies the core function of initiation as a procedure meant to deal with the enforcement of superego demands. In Bettelheim's study, initiation is a constitutive part of subjectivity.[7]

Typically, in puberty rites such as circumcision, the act of mutilation of the organ confers a particular potency on the organ. Bettelheim's study of initiation rites, *Symbolic Wounds* (1954), shows the ubiquity of initiation even for those without a formal link to a religious community, a family or other forms of community. We could say then that initiation imposes itself

---

[6] For a fascinating dissection of Miller's more recent political commitments, see the first chapter of Gabriel Tupinambá's *The Desire of Psychoanalysis* (2021).

[7] In Bettelheim's *Symbolic Wounds* (1971) he considers the contemporary period as conditioned by a crisis of initiation. He points out that even schizophrenic children seek spontaneous rites of initiation and bodily mutilation we find a deeply penetrating insight that links up with Deleuze and Guattari's anti-Oedipal theory of capitalism producing schizophrenic effects on subjects. As we see in Badiou's theory of "initiation without initiation"—this spontaneous form of initiation is the predominant way initiation occurs today, untethered from rites, rituals, and traditions.

as a subjective demand and as a necessity. Bettelheim observes that even schizophrenic children develop the need for initiation rites and often impose them spontaneously. In a critique of the standard Freudian theory of initiation as symbolic castration rooted in what Freud called "neurotic castration anxiety," Bettelheim (1971) argues instead that initiation rites are to be understood as rooted in envy of the other's sexes organs.

Going against Freud's proposal of penis envy, Bettelheim argues that the human subject possesses "polyvalent sexual predispositions." He leans on Jung's theory of early sexuality over Freud's "polymorphous perversity" (148–150) to make this claim. Bettelheim thus argues that polyvalent sexual tendencies; that is, non-normative sexual attractions are the seeds of social and sexual behavior and are experienced at a young age but soon prohibited and repressed by the norms of society as the child ages (pp. 149–151).

Initiation rites are very often enacted across cultures to satisfy this precise longing for polyvalent sexual predispositions, and Bettelheim explores a myriad of examples of rites in ancient societies to the contemporary period that offer ritual opportunities for members of the community to inhabit the other sexes sexual organs. Most often, rites involve games and ceremonies in which the boys and the men can experience femininity during the rite before they eventually return to a more masculine state. The effect of the initiation rites is not to bind the initiate with the community primarily but to forge an independence of the subject. Moreover, through that independence, a binding with the community comes secondarily. A world bereft of initiation is one wherein subjectivity loses the necessary forms of independence that bring about the possibility of collective binding and solidarity. A crisis of initiation is a profound subjective problem in our world.

References

Bettelheim, B. (1971). *Symbolic Wounds: Puberty Rites and the Envious Male.* Collier Books.

Lacan, J. (1938). *La famille in Encyclopédie française* (R. Klein, Trans., vol. 8). A. de Monzie, Editor.

Lacan, J. (1970). Allocution prononcée pour la clôture du Congrès de l'École freudienne de Paris le 19 avril 1970 par son directeur in Scilicet, 4° trimestre 1970 (n° 2/3, pp. 391–399).

Lacan, J. (1971). *Seminar XVIII on a Discourse That Might Not Be a Semblant* (C. McCarthy, Trans., pp. 38–39).

Lacan, J. (1972). *Discours de Jacques Lacan à l'Université de Milan (The Capitalist Discourse)* (R. Klein, Trans.). See www.Freud2Lacan.com

Lacan, J. (1993). *Seminar III the Psychoses 1955–1956* (R. Grigg, Trans.). W.W. Norton and Company.

Lacan, J. (2006). *Écrits: The Complete First Edition* (B. Fink, Trans.). W.W. Norton & Company.

Lacan, J. (2007). *The Other Side of Psychoanalysis: The Seminar of Jacques Lacan Book XVII* (R. Grigg, Trans.). W.W. Norton and Company.

Lacan, J. (2017). *Formations of the Unconscious: The Seminar of Jacques Lacan, Book V* (R. Grigg, Trans.). Polity Press.

Laurent, E., & Miller, J. (1998). The Other Who Does Not Exist and His Ethical Committees. *Almanac of Psychoanalysis, 1*, 15–35.

McGowan, T. (2016). *Capitalism and desire: The psychic cost of free markets.* Columbia University Press.

Miller, J. (2019). *Paradigms of Jouissance: Three Interventions by Jacques-Alain Miller* (R. Litten, Trans. and Ed., Psychoanalytical Notebooks No. 34). Karnac Books.

Moncayo, R. (2012). *Emptiness of Oedipus: Identification and Non-Identification in Lacanian Psychoanalysis.* Routledge.

Svolos, T. (2017). *Psychoanalysis in the Twenty-First Century.* Routledge.

Tupinambá, G. (2021). *The Desire of Psychoanalysis: Exercises in Lacanian Thinking.* Northwestern University Press.

Vanheule, S. (2016). Capitalist Discourse, Subjectivity and Lacanian Psychoanalysis. *Frontiers in Psychology, 09.* https://doi.org/10.3389/fpsyg.2016.01948

Zupančič, A. (2000). *Ethics of the Real: Kant and Lacan.* Verso Books.

CHAPTER 6

Initiation: René Girard and Alain Badiou

Abstract This chapter analyzes two preeminent contemporary philosophers, René Girard and Alain Badiou, and looks at how both thinkers understand the broader crisis of initiation facing our present age. It focuses on how both thinkers theorize the Oedipus complex and the Oedipal problem from a distinctive anti-humanist point of view. While the two thinkers under consideration are vastly different in how they propose dealing with this problem, we conclude by examining the shortcomings and the important insights both thinkers offer to the problem.

Keywords Alain Badiou • René Girard • Mimetic desire • Initiation without initiation • Initiation • Emancipation • Oedipus

Rarely are the two preeminent French philosophers René Girard, a philosopher whose "mimetic desire" theory has hugely influenced both academia and Silicon Valley,[1] and Alain Badiou, the Marxist philosopher who

---

[1] See the book *What Tech Calls Thinking* (2020) by Adrian Daub to get a better idea of Girard's profound influence on neoliberal organizational theory and Silicon Valley business culture. Peter Thiel, the founder of PayPal, and one of the wealthiest individuals in Silicon Valley (and the world) is an outspoken Girardian and has created a charitable organization meant to further study mimetic desire within organizations and institutional life.

© The Author(s), under exclusive license to Springer Nature
Switzerland AG 2022
D. Tutt, *Psychoanalysis and the Politics of the Family: The Crisis of
Initiation*, The Palgrave Lacan Series,
https://doi.org/10.1007/978-3-030-94070-6_6

has refined a comprehensive philosophy of the "subject" over the past 45 years,[2] put into conversation with one another. Both thinkers assist us in thinking about the crisis of initiation in distinct ways. But, not surprisingly, they propose radically divergent remedies to the subjective crisis of our time.

But both Girard and Badiou are committed to an anti-humanist reading of psychoanalysis; that is, they hold the view, similar to Lacan, that psychic repression does not arise from some structural imprint of the human mind and that the Oedipus complex is not a matter of consciousness. Girard's critique of psychoanalysis in *Violence and the Sacred* (1972) opens a new way of reading the Oedipus complex that is not grounded in a necessarily sexual theory of desire, and he completely scraps the Freudian theory of repression. We will begin with an analysis of Girard's critique of the Oedipus complex and then turn to Badiou's analysis of the Oedipus complex and the crisis of initiation. We will conclude with a consideration and assessment of the different strategies for overcoming the initiation crisis they propose.

Girard critiques the Freudian conception of the Oedipus complex in ways far different from Lacan. For Girard, the Oedipus complex is a humanist theory that relies on a subject of consciousness, and these presuppositions of Freud are both errors in Girard's view. Girard writes,

> In the final analysis, what I object to most is Freud's obstinate attachment—despite all appearances—to a philosophy of consciousness. The mythical aspect of Freudianism is founded on the conscious knowledge of patricidal and incestuous desire; only a brief flash of consciousness, to be sure, a bright wedge of light between the darkness of the first identifications and the unconscious—but consciousness all the same. Freud's stubborn attachment to this consciousness compels him to abandon both logic and credibility. He first assumes this consciousness and then gets rid of it in a kind of safe-deposit box, the unconscious. In effect he is saying: ego can suppress all consciousness of a patricidal and incestuous desire only if at one time ego truly experienced it. Ergo sum. (p. 187)

The Freudian Oedipus complex is critiqued here as a "humanist" theory that relies on "consciousness" of the father—like Deleuze and Guattari's critique, which we elaborate on in the next chapter—in a way that is

---

[2] Alain Badiou is considered by many as the foremost philosopher in the world today. His thought comes at the end of the renaissance in philosophical thought that emerged in post-war France, and his thought synthesizes strains of twentieth-century French philosophy, from Sartre to Deleuze to Lacan.

idealist and metaphysical. For Girard, psychoanalysis is right to put the father in a central place of psychic life in our modern epoch, but he proposes a different account of the nature of the crisis of the symbolic law. For Girard, the "Oedipus complex appears most plausible in a society in which the father's authority has been greatly weakened but not completely destroyed; that is, in Western society during the course of recent centuries" (p. 199). Girard thus recognizes the crisis of the social superego we have been tracking throughout this book, but he locates this crisis as *a transhistorical crisis of any social order facing an absence of rites and of the religious* more generally:

> It is not law, in any conceivable form, that is responsible for the tensions and alienation besetting modern man; rather, it is the increasing lack of law. The perpetual denunciation of the law arises from a typically modern sense of resentment—a feedback of desire that purports to be directed against the law but one that is actually aimed at the model-obstacle whose dominant position the subject stubbornly refuses to acknowledge. The more frenzied the mimetic process becomes, caught up in the confusion of constantly changing forms, the more unwilling men are to recognize that they have made an obstacle of the model and a model of the obstacle. Here we encounter a true "unconscious," and one that can obviously assume many forms. (p. 199)

Theoretical concepts such as the Oedipus complex are only possible in a symbolic order that is born of the scapegoat mechanism (Girard, 1978), that is, of a collective violence that is always at the mercy of reciprocal violence (p. 703). Thus, psychoanalysis is correct to point to the crisis of what Lacan called the Name-of-the-Father, or the pluralization of the Oedipus complex, as a unique problem that emerges from the split law or double bind that marks the contemporary social order. In Girard's view, the superego is nothing more than a resumption of identification with the father, now appearing chronologically after the Oedipus complex rather than before it. The double bind occurs in the superego injunction, "You may not be like this (your father) ... some things are his prerogative," Freud is clearly referring to the mother in Girard's view. He argues this double aspect of the ego ideal in Freudian thought "derives from the fact that the ego ideal had the task of repressing the Oedipus complex; indeed, it is to that revolutionary event that it owes its existence" (p. 191).

Girard's solution to the impasse of the double bind is not to move with the intensities and flows of desire that come about in its wake, as Deleuze and Guattari aim to do; such an approach is naively trying to find a "peaceful coexistence between the extremes of delirium" (pp. 86–87). Girard rather opts for a more conservative treatment of the crisis of the double bind, or the crisis of initiation because he sees its effects as primarily giving way to mimetic reciprocal violence. He argues the individual who adjusts to this condition by neutralizing the double bind, or by concealing the violence of mimetic desire is the only subject capable of bringing an end to the crisis of mimetic violence. On the other hand, the maladjusted individual is the one who has refused to conceal the crisis.

This signifies the importance of religion for Girard's approach to overcoming the double bind of Oedipus. Girard's theory here should be read as a reparative treatment and strategy for managing the crisis of initiation because he argues that religion offers the most refined and sophisticated treatment of concealing mimetic violence through rites which *enact a symbolic substitution mechanism*. In Girard's view, religions today no longer need to call upon the scapegoat mechanism as they have pushed it down through the repetition of rites—ceremonies, holidays, rites of initiation, and so on.

Where Girard differs from Freud and Lacan is in his theory of how mimetic desire perpetuates; he argues that mimetic desire detaches desire from any predetermined object, whereas the Oedipus complex fixes desire on the maternal object. He writes, "the mimetic concept eliminates all conscious knowledge of patricide-incest, and even all desire for it as such; the Freudian proposition, by contrast, is based entirely on a consciousness of this desire" (p. 189). Freud's definition of the superego presupposes something quite different from a mythical consciousness of rivalry; he rather grounds desire on the model's identification with the obstacle, an identification that goes unperceived by the disciple. This perceived shortcoming of Freudianism leads Girard to juxtapose his theory of mimetic desire to the Freudian theory of Oedipus. In the mimetic definition of desire, Girard can account for rivalry without the Oedipus complex, as mimetic desire brings forth an unlimited number of doubles without referring to myth or to the processes of Oedipal identification and working-through within the nuclear family.

In the theory of mimetic desire, the conflict arises as a fundamental trait of all human relations, "the universal double bind of imitated desires" (p. 192). Rivalry does not arise because of the fortuitous convergence of two desires on a single object (as in the Freudian account of Oedipus); rather, the subject desires the object because the rival desires it. In desiring an object, the rival alerts the subject to the desirability of the object. The rival, then, serves as a model for the subject, not only regarding such secondary matters as style and opinions but also, and more essentially, regarding desires (pp. 154–155).

It is important to note that Girard's entire theory of the symbolic order is born from what he calls the "scapegoat mechanism," that is, "a collective violence that is always at the mercy of reciprocal violence" (Girard, 1978, p. 95). The Oedipus complex is the disguised representation of the scapegoat or sacrificial victim that each of us must internalize and then externalize. But Girard goes even further and attempts to show how his idea of the scapegoat mechanism is already present in Freud's thought in the very movement and logic of the ego Ideal itself. For Girard, the leap to a pre-conscious relation to the transcendental father in psychoanalytic thought isn't necessary to account for the outbreak of mimetic desire. He thus throws into question the very status of Freud's idea that ambivalent affects are the heart of the subject's relation to the Oedipus complex.

In a short, yet highly relevant essay for our purposes, titled "The Son's Aleatory Identity in Today's World" (2007), the philosopher Alain Badiou brings the Oedipal drama into his own philosophical system. He focuses on the larger question of the crisis of youth identity and the defective Oedipal situation, and his account of Oedipus is close to that of Freud. He even states explicitly that his reading is a re-reading of Freud's myths in *Totem and Taboo* and *Moses and Monotheism*, but the key difference between them is the way in which Badiou develops the myths as a distinctive, albeit defective, dialectic. In Badiou's revision of the Oedipal myth according to Freud, the first act of the drama consists of the son's fratricidal murder of the father of the horde, to stop his possessive hording of all the women. In the second act, the son sublimates a new father onto the symbolic that functions as the Law of society (p. 77). In the third and final act, the son confronts the father once again, and after undergoing a brutal bodily initiation with the father, enters the reign of mutual love with the father, and the Oedipal dialectic has reached its end point.

These three acts form a dialectic that repeats and creates a *necessary* basis for resolving the impasse of the father-to-son relation. The son must pass through these stages not in linear but in logical time: aggressiveness, followed by submission to the Law, and the Christian reign of mutual love. The son's identity today is thus, according to Badiou, deprived of the father of the real and the symbolic (the first two acts) resulting in the son's "permanent adolescence." To apply religious symbolism, the son is in a type of purgatory where his initiation into the reign of mutual love is impossible. Badiou refers to this type of existence as an "initiation without initiation" and in an imaginary relation to the father. The son, lacking a passage or confrontation with the first two acts is reduced to what Badiou refers to as a "subjective body," but unlike his typical conception of body, the son is relegated to a "permanent adolescence." Ultimately, Badiou locates the impasse of the son's body at the site of the "democratic" state and in the space of representation, which has been "gravely affected in its symbolic capacity" which creates an identity instability of the son.

Badiou will argue that the strained Oedipal dynamics of our time amount to "a profound symptom of a problem that affects the State" (p. 78). There are fundamental differences between Badiou and Lacan on the question of the subject. For Lacan, the subject exists upon entry into the chain of signifiers, whereas for Badiou, the subject requires incorporation into a truth body and an undergoing of fidelity to an Event, which is more generally understood as a subject thought in the context of language (Lacan) compared to a subject thought in terms of a world (Badiou).

Badiou's subject is always a becoming-subject in each context. The Badiouian conception of the subject is thus always composed with the material of the situation but is posited beyond the individual whereas Lacan's notion of subjectivation, which he defines in the traversal of the fundamental fantasy, Badiou's subject begins with incorporation into the process of a truth. In Badiou's essay on the son's aleatory identity, the son is reduced to a body and unable to become a subject because he is deprived of initiation with the father, however, he identifies three body positions of the son today. The first body for the son is what Badiou calls the "perverted body," whereby the initiation with the father is deprived and the son, taking on his body at the end of the previous dialectic acts out the aggressiveness he is deprived of. The perverted body revels in the failed dialectic and seeks to simulate an initiation with the father of the horde through body piercing, violence, drugs, and so on. Ultimately, this form of initiation must be understood as distinct from the more is predominant form of initiation, what Badiou calls the "meritorious body"—following the market's demand to "Succeed!"

The meritorious body is still deprived of a proper initiation with the father of the symbolic that leaves the son in a state of immobility because, as Badiou remarks, "the market is forever immobile, so that which produces Law becomes an immobility" (p. 78). The third body is what Badiou calls the "sacrificed body" that remains tethered to tradition, mortified to live with what a new body can support. This body is the one of religious tradition and following a conservative injunction, trapped with a father of the weak symbolic Law that is ultimately one that does not provide any adequate level of authority, which the sacrificed body desires.

In considering the question of the three bodies of the son, is Badiou not missing a fourth body? If the meritorious body constitutes the predominant body of the market, that must follow the injunction of the social superego, which to the extent that it demands the subject it demands a belief in its very efficacy, a compulsion tied to success and accomplishment, or what Han calls the performance society. But is not capitalism now creating conditions for even the meritorious body to face exclusion from even minimal participation in the market? There should be a fourth body, what I call the "non-meritorious body" that is excluded from the market, thrown to the assembly line, forced into unemployment, not eligible for college loans, and outside of the meritorious society.

This "non-meritorious body" is still thrown to the Law of the market, but his capacity is rendered doubly immobile, both by his lack of access to the market and in his symbolic relation to the market. In all three (or four) bodies, Badiou's proposal of a non-dialectizable body relegates the son to a supra-adolescence that is reduced to immobility based on the anonymity of the Law. As Badiou remarks, "the law, because the market produces it, is forever immobile, so that which produces Law always produces immobility."

The impasse the sons face is not located in a defective dialectical initiation with the father. Badiou's claim is that this impasse must be resolved ultimately by the destruction of the market, but in this destruction, what type of mediator appears to "initiate" the son? What enables the son to "live for an Idea" as Badiou is fond of saying? We find in Badiou's "perverted body" and in what we call the "non-meritorious body" two subjective positions that can break with the Law of the market.[3] The question of

---

[3] A major theme in thinking the contemporary class struggle in today's time for Badiou and for Slavoj Žižek has been the proposal of the "nomadic proletariat," who are not proletarians in the strict Marxian sense but are more in line with the *lumpenproletariat*, given their labor is not within productive labor in a formal sense. The non-meritorious body is akin the nomadic proletariat, and we examine how this category of class can be thought on a far wider basis in the chapter "The Political Stakes of the Social Superego."

the son's becoming a subject is one that strikes at the heart of revolution and the necessity of revolution:

> Maybe the sons of today, in their identity instability, are the symptom of a profound process that affects the State. It is perhaps in our sons that we can read the result of that long-abandoned prediction of Marx, the decay of the State. Marx had ascribed it under the sign of communism, of revolution, to that which will restore the complete dialectic of our sons in the element of equality and versatile universal knowledge. Do we have today the reactive and decomposed version of this decay? The "democratic" state is in any case gravely affected in its symbolic capacity. Perhaps by our sons are we confronted more than ever with the strategic choice between two conflicting modes of the State: communism or barbarism. (pp. 82–83)

The defective Oedipal dialectic is tied to a crisis of the state, as well as the institution of the family, as both are in alignment with the state. While Badiou does not rely on Althusser's ideological state apparatus in his conception of the state, he turns to Marx's early formulations of the state as already undergoing a process of continual withering away. In such a reading, the family, and by extension, this potentially renewed Oedipal dialectic comes is conditioned by love. As Badiou writes, "love is an obstinate struggle against separation"; thus, the erosion of the state and the family by barbarism or communism, requires a stabilizing procedure, that is, love. Love is the stabilizing procedure that "should organize the withering away of the family." As Badiou writes:

> I think that assigning the family as love's obligatory finality creates considerable difficulties for love. In the same way, making the takeover of State power the inevitable objective politics creates considerable difficulties for politics. (pp. 50–51)

Badiou's notion of a renewed Oedipal dialectic is in line with Marx's vision of a "withering away of the state," and this procedure of love, Badiou argues, "is not at all, as people think, to construct a family but to invent forms that free the scene of the Two from family egoism" (p. 51). What Badiou thus advocates in the face of the condition of "initiation without initiation" is a new thinking of love as initiation, a new form of thinking the family as a revolutionary agency.

Although Girard advocates a conservative treatment of mimetic desire, he also aims for the restoration of a functioning law, a form of initiation which would produce an efficacious result. But for Girard, initiation can only be resorted via a transcendental quality of the system, that is, the establishment of new rites and myths that can provide necessary conceal-ments of mimetic desire. Only by opting for a sanctified, legitimate form of violence and preventing it from becoming an object of disputes and recriminations can the system save itself from the vicious circle of revenge in Girard's (1977) view (p. 24).

Badiou diagnoses the problem well; he says that the social superego and the marketization of everyday life has resulted in a stunted form of initia-tion. Badiou understands initiation as the creation of a new desire—that is, he remains true to a Lacanian theory of the subject. At the same time, he recognizes that the state has been the primary purveyor of initiation and this initiation has come in the form of compulsory drafting into warfare. Today it is the market that has produced a paralysis of initiation, the only form of initiation worth striving for is a revolutionary one, one that can forge a completely new relation to the political.

What are the practical consequences of Badiou's and Girard's insights in terms of the politics of the family? For Badiou, the first important insight has to do with the way that the position of the father has resulted in a completely inverted form of initiation: "it is the father nowadays who tends to envy the sons jouissance, and the reconciliation of father and son can only come about by the infantilization of the father," Badiou writes. What effects the family today is this crisis of the Oedipal dynamic given that at the level of desire, something has broken, the subject (in this case the son, but we can just as easily invoke the daughter) faces a violence of being relegated to the third stage in the Oedipal drama, which we dis-cussed in the last chapter. This purgatory results in a violence for both father and son/subject at the same time. The four bodies that we have proposed in this chapter are each, in their own way, a response to this reversed Oedipal dynamic.

Girard's theory of mimetic desire and his wider work are complemen-tary to Badiou's insights apropos the family because he aims to mitigate the violence of this crisis, but he does so by introducing more consistent rites, a turn to religion, and so on. Girard's theory of mimetic desire makes for a practical guidebook for managing the family as an organization that can set the scapegoat mechanism down, locate it, and prevent it from becoming a negative reliance of the family. In fact, the Girardian method, within the family, might even be a solution to the Oedipal conflicts that emerge within the family.

As we saw for Girard, the Oedipus complex itself, even in Freud's formulation, is a theory meant to resolve violence at the origin of the drama of any human community. Girard is interested in creating modern techniques for doing the same thing, specifically by locating how the technologies form religious traditions can further this end. Where Girard's orientation falls short in our view is in two ways: the first is that Girard sees emancipatory movements such as Marxism as themselves falling sway to the scapegoat mechanism. In an interview, Girard (1987) comments:

> We must refuse all scapegoats that Freud offered us: the father, the law, etc. We must refuse the scapegoats that Marx offers: the bourgeoisie, the capitalists, etc. They prepare the way for the omnipresent victim who has already been prepared since time immemorial. (pp. 294–295)

More broadly, Girardian theory possess a certain strategic and practical power for groups in the sense that the scapegoat mechanism does indeed emerge within groups and in some situations, it is necessary to mitigate, neutralize, and alleviate the scapegoat. However, this approach to the "scapegoat mechanism" when taken at a broader societal level can also result in a reactionary affirmation for the status quo. The second way the Girardian theory falls short to the problems we aim to address, especially of the paradox of liberation, is that he is not interested in any dialectical approach to social or political antagonisms, that is, to furthering social and political antagonisms that force a contradiction or a break or rupture with the status quo, for example. Thus, at the social and political levels, Girard's solutions for mitigating social violence through support for religious institutions may be valuable but not in conditions of late capitalism in which the very forces of hyper-marketization are not transcendable through religious community. The problem of violence is not the most central dynamic that must be overcome and the competitive social relations that capitalism foments are not the most central driver of violence in our world. Marxism possesses a far more robust method for addressing structural violence than the Girardian theory contains.

Given that Girard does not present a viable theory of justice in which oppressed groups can find a path toward freedom and greater justice without being accused of becoming victims in their act of demanding justice, Girard's thought is made complicit with status quo liberal politics and even worse than that, with forms of neo-feudal tech monopoly. Girard is a strong critic of capitalist competition, seeing in competition the source of the emergence of mimetic desire itself. As a result of this aversion to competition, much of the structure of Girardian companies, such as the companies that Peter Thiel runs, are effectively structured in such a way that they have foreclosed competition entirely. Schullenberg (2016) has argued this approach to organization has made Thiel and other Silicon Valley tech CEOs that find influence in Girard, effectively furthering a neo-feudal business strategy.[4]

Badiou's approach to the political dimension of the politics of the family is dialectical and emancipatory. He proposes that only in a revolutionary new configuration of the state, precisely a more egalitarian state, can a comprehensive solution be found to this subjective crisis. We follow this proposal in more detail in the chapter "The Political Stakes of the Social Superego."

REFERENCES

Badiou, A. (2007). *The Son's Aleatory Identity in Today's World* (Vol. 32). Lacanian Ink.

Girard, R. (1977). *Violence and the Sacred* (P. Gregory, Trans.) (p. 187). John Hopkins University Press Baltimore.

Girard, R. (1978). *"To Double Business Bound": Essays on Literature, Mimesis, and Anthropology* (pp. 84–120). The Johns Hopkins University Press.

Girard, R. (1987). *Things Hidden Since the Foundation of the World* (M. Metter, Trans.). Stanford University Press.

Schullenberg, G. (2016, November). The Scapegoating Machine? *New Inquiry.*

---

[4] For a deeper analysis of this claim that Girard's mimetic desire furthers neo-feudal organizational structures, please see Schullenberg, Geoff, "The Scapegoating Machine?"

CHAPTER 7

Accelerate the Social Superego? Critique of Deleuze and Guattari

Abstract This chapter examines the legacy of the radical and liberatory work *Anti-Oedipus: Capitalism and Schizophrenia* (1972). This chapter argues the revolutionary anti-Oedipal philosophy and critique of the family developed over this two-decade-long project has not been borne out by developments of late capitalism. Although many of the strategies of praxis developed in this work are valuable—and we discuss them—we argue the project fell sway to the wall of ultra-liberalism, which led to a dampening of the intensity of the project. We conclude with an examination of how Deleuze, in his later work, overcomes some of these political limitations.

Keywords Deleuze and Guattari • Initiation • Incest • Ultra-liberalism • Anti-Oedipus

In late twentieth-century radical philosophy and psychoanalysis, the *Anti-Oedipus: Capitalism and Schizophrenia* (1972) series, which ended with a work titled *What Is Philosophy?* in 1991, stands out as arguably the most influential set of texts to address the intersection of Marx and Freud. Although deeply critical of Freud, and less so of Marx, Gilles Deleuze and Félix Guattari's *Anti-Oedipus* series marks an essential contribution to the problem of liberation and the wider dynamic of the social superego we have developed thus far. In what follows, we read Deleuze and Guattari

© The Author(s), under exclusive license to Springer Nature   81
Switzerland AG 2022
D. Tutt, *Psychoanalysis and the Politics of the Family: The Crisis of Initiation*, The Palgrave Lacan Series,
https://doi.org/10.1007/978-3-030-94070-6_7

into the problems that concern us: the family, subjective initiation, the social superego, and the paradox of liberation. We conclude this argument and extend it to the next chapter that the anti-Oedipal critique has faced a wall of liberalism and its strategies have not been borne out by history.

Anti-Oedipus was released in 1973, a symbolically significant year, marked by the dawn of the economy going off the gold standard and the concomitant rise of early financial-dominated capitalism. Echoing the Frankfurt School and the work of communist psychoanalyst Wilhelm Reich, a critique of the family form is central to the wider project in this work. They aim for nothing less than an all-out critique and assault on the Oedipal desiring system itself, which they claim is the primary "metaphysics of capitalism."

Deleuze and Guattari develop a "transcendental" alternative to the metaphysics of Oedipal capitalism. The best way to understand what they mean by desire is when they write, "desire makes its entry with the general collapse of the question *what does it mean* in favor of *how does it work?*" The unconscious is founded on a transcendental instead of a metaphysical basis and it is nonfigurative rather than imaginary, which is to say that for them the unconscious is directly linked into social production, it is immediately tied into the earth, which is the first "socius" (p. 109).

In their analysis, Oedipus is an agency of the state, of paranoia and power long before being delegated to the family (p. xx), which tracks very closely with what the Marxist and socialist-feminist tradition maintains. Wilhelm Reich, a major influence of the materialist turn within psychoanalysis—and whose *Mass Psychology of Fascism* (1933) located the rise of fascism in Germany with the repressed desire emanating from the bourgeois family—is arguably the most important psychoanalyst for this project next to Lacan. In Reich's view (1980), the repression of the family is *the bulwark to revolutionary potential* and to the wider acquiescence to repressive social codes. Deleuze and Guattari will develop the idea that "desire is productive" from a reading of the unconscious as a construct that is totally unaware of persons as such but driven primarily by "partial objects." This insight is linked to the important psychoanalytic idea of "polymorphous perversity" or the pre-social period of a child's life in which they experience pleasure that is fulfilling to organs and not caught within social taboos and norms. This more elemental state of the subject drives Deleuze and Guattari to put forward the "body without organs" as a mode of subjective return to this condition in which different erogenous zones and what they call "desiring machines" govern.

The text builds on the American cybernetician Gregory Bateson's idea of the "double bind," which they locate as the central dynamic at play in the Oedipus complex. Deleuze and Guattari argue, rightly, that the fundamental double bind of capitalist life is Oedipal desire, and the contradictory way Oedipal desire operates on the symbolic law of the father. The double bind of Oedipus sets its own trap, in the law of the father: "do as I say, not as I do." The idea of the double bind comes out of anthropological work done by Bronisław Malinowski, who discovered a social order in the Trobriand Islands, in Melanesia, where the father is not the authority figure, but the maternal uncle is. In such an arrangement of authority within the family there was an absence of neurosis because the father doesn't function as a contradiction but serves over only sublimation, not both sublimation and repression. The double bind of Western civilizations finds its historical legacy in the Abrahamic paternal authority structures, which position the father as a figure of authority over the symbolic law and over sublimation. It was these anthropological and ethnographic insights of non-Oedipal desire structures that would lead Lacan to fundamentally *de-mythify* Oedipus and Deleuze and Guattari's *Anti-Oedipus* should be read in a similar way.

As it pertains to initiation, the authors have several important insights to offer. In their study of the history of desiring machines and different social formations throughout history, they build off the work of the anthropologist Claude-Lévi Strauss. In a way quite similar to Bruno Bettelheim's study of initiation, Deleuze and Guattari find that initiatory rites in tribal societies tended to deal with the body in a way that treats the subject less like a "person" and more like a "body." That is, the Oedipal dynamic and its metaphysics impose personhood as a type of representational violence done to the subject:

Initiation societies compose the pieces of a body, which are at the same time sensory organs, anatomical parts, and joints. Prohibitions (see not, speak not) apply to those who, in a given state or on a given occasion, are deprived of the right to enjoy a collectively invested organ. The mythologies sing of organs-partial objects and their relations with a full body that repels or attracts them: vaginas riveted on the woman's body, an immense penis shared by the men, an independent anus that assigns itself a body without anus. (p. 92)

What marks the rise of the Oedipal social order is the way it privatizes the organs, and the first organ that has been taken outside of the social field was the anus. Initiation rites are thus in crisis constitutively so within the modern bourgeois order in their reading. We disagree with this point because we see in Oedipus a source of psychic liberation, not a completely reactionary process.

They agree with Engels' argument in *Origins of the Bourgeois Family* that kinship relations in pre-modern and pre-capitalist societies were a form of praxis; that is, the family is a social arrangement, not a filial arrangement. This insight means that the family can take different forms and have more liberatory expressions, it is not merely an invention of the bourgeoisie. However, when the modern bourgeois family emerges, the parental figures are inductors, not organizers of desire. The family is thus a structural re-routing of desiring production, and the parental imagos are not the *real* inductors, they are rendered transcendent (p. 92). Oedipal desire, in the modern bourgeois social order is thus not invented by the unconscious but is a discursive invention of the state and of other forms of social power. They are keen to locate psychoanalysts-as-an-institution in capitalist society that is also granted a great deal of power in legitimating the Oedipal system itself:

> It is only little by little that he makes the familial romance, on the contrary, into a mere dependence on Oedipus, and that he neuroticizes everything in the unconscious at the same time as he oedipalizes, and closes the familial triangle over the entire unconscious. (pp. 54–55)

Anti-Oedipus takes aim at the conservative potential inherent in Freud's work, locating this tendency at the point when Freud discovered the autonomous value to psychic repression as a condition of culture acting against the incestuous drives. Psychoanalysis can't see beyond the repression it posits as necessary and comes to see its solutions as the only viable ones to the problem it has established.

Our first critique of this text, despite its many deeply significant insights into liberation and revolution, is that its diagnosis places far too much of the onus of Oedipus on psychoanalysis and psychoanalysts. Psychoanalysis no longer has the institutional power it once had in the '60s and '70s due to the ripping apart of the welfare state social service protections under neoliberal rule. In the next chapter, we argue that an analysis of the way liberalism furthers its political theories of justice and citizenship are far more central to the perpetuation of the metaphysics of Oedipus today than psychoanalysis was back in the '60s and '70s. They write:

> Instead of participating in an undertaking that will bring about genuine liberation, psychoanalysis is taking part in the work of bourgeois repression at its most far-reaching level, that is to say, keeping European humanity harnessed to the yoke of daddy-mommy and making no effort to do away with this problem once and for all. (p. 50)

This reading of the liberatory potential of psychoanalysis is uncharitable and hyperbolic. How can the yoke of "daddy-mommy" be extinguished precisely? There is an excessive libertinism that is admirable in this work, but at times, it is too excessive. The best example of this excessiveness is found in Deleuze and Guattari's claim that "incest is impossible" because to truly consider the problem of incest is to understand the prior problematic that gives rise to it, namely, the invention of the "person" as such.

In their eyes, one cannot enjoy the person and the name the person is given at the same time; that is, a person is an oppressive social invention that cannot be situated as separate from "intensive flows." What is repressed prior to any act of incest is the intensity of the "germinal influx," and it is the germinal influx that "conditions all representation" and as such it is the representative of desire. Oedipal desire represses and blocks this better, more liberatory access to the germinal intensity of the earth:

> Incest is only the retroactive effect of the repressing representation on the repressed representative: the representation disfigures or displaces this representative against which it is directed; it projects onto the representative, categories, rendered discernible, that it has established; it applies to the representative terms that did not exist before the alliance organized the positive and the negative into a system in extension—the representation reduces the representative to what is blocked in this system. (p. 165)

This dense passage presents us with a seemingly out-of-touch philosophy and praxis, which is furthering a transcendental alternative to a system of Oedipal desire which is so total that to escape or to perform a "line of flight" from it, one faces a massive castration. If incest is only the "retroactive effect of the repressing representation" of Oedipus this calls for a total overthrow of Oedipus. We thus agree with René Girard's critique of *Anti-Oedipus* that in aiming to circumvent the problem of castration, they only intensify it. Girard suggests that "the omnipotence of desiring production is absolutely indistinguishable, in practice, from a radical castration" (p. 95).

This leads to our second critique: they argue the flows and circuits of desire must avoid becoming "territorialized" by Oedipus, a prospect they associate with fascism. Fascism builds a territory of desire and builds up and affirms the metaphysics of Oedipus in a "molar" fashion as opposed to the more liberatory "molecular" praxis they advocate. In one example, they note the literary figure of Jack Kerouac, as he aged and settled his road travel books, he began to develop a distinct American fascism, retiring in an alcoholic stupor with his mother. But in our era that is dominated by the social superego, the very idea of "de-territorializing" desire to produce a "line of flight" from Oedipus no longer makes sense as a clear mark of subjective freedom from the double bind. As we developed earlier, the social superego operates on the logic of a double bind that is not reliant on the law of the father. Deleuze and Guattari's emphasis on flows and circuits of desire requiring movement and freedom from the territorializing encroachment of Oedipus is no longer a sensible proposal.

The concept "line of flight" presupposes an outside, or what in Lacanian thought is often called an "extimate" space of psychic life, but there is no pure outside. Furthermore, they scrap dialectics entirely and replace it with a different logic of resistance and a novel theory of groups. They propose replacing psychoanalysis with Schizoanalysis, which is based on the proposal that a naturalized transcendental conception of the unconscious, as opposed to the metaphysical unconscious as founded by Freud, is indeed clinically possible. While this would consume the bulk of Félix Guattari's later work, it is important to note that Schizoanalysis remained for the most part a speculative proposition and not an extant institutional force.[1] Yet the core wager of Schizoanalysis remains a provocative horizon for the era of the predominance of the social superego and a capitalist system in which Oedipus is delayed and inefficacious, namely, that collective group formations no longer need the transcendent figure of the leader to sustain their cohesion. In this way, Deleuze and Guattari offer a political

---

[1] The legacy of Guattari's thought today does not seem to reside within the clinic, although some Lacanian analysts utilize many of his insights, but more in radical philosophical circles and militant political groups.

theory of groups and solidarity across groups that transcends mere clinical contributions and contains a wealth of insights for emancipatory politics.[2]

What remains of utmost importance in the "Schizoanalytic" model is the analysis that desire is constituted on social repression and that this is the primary source of repression, as opposed to psychic repression. If all repression is socially derived, and not individually derived, if neuroses are always a social phenomenon, forming identity around the signifier of one's own identity risks getting caught in the web of the signifier as opposed to the sign. Deleuze and Guattari thus contribute to a strong critique of identity politics in this analysis of desire and repression.

The vocation of the sign is to produce desire, engineering it in every direction and it is important to locate desire around signs. This is a project that is dependent on three different syntheses: (1) The connective synthesis that connects and unites partial objects rather than extant identity blocs or groups; (2) the conjunctive synthesis, or a reactionary synthesis that associates libidinal discharge with an identification of the ego that produces a subject in line with machinic desire; and (3) the disjunctive synthesis which operates on the logic that "everything divides, but into itself" (p. 117). Of these three syntheses, it is the disjunctive syntheses that produces the double-bind logic that operates on the premise that identity is not tethered to a metaphysical necessity but is *created in a material transcendental process*. In the idea of the disjunctive synthesis, collective group formations no longer need the transcendent figure of the leader to sustain their cohesion. This presents an important insight apropos revolutionary praxis; group liberation must locate the signs that "demonstrate the existence of an unconscious libidinal investment of sociohistorical production, distinct from the conscious investments coexisting with it" (p. 98).

Rather than submitting to the Oedipal paradigm which halts desire processes upon an identity, the "Schizoanalytic" praxis insists that alternative forms of identification with signs that point to unconscious desire become a new mode of praxis. How to locate unconscious desire becomes the basis for the creation of a new transcendental of the unconscious. Thus, instead of thinking identification with an ego ideal or ideal ego (the

---

[2] It is worth noting the profound legacy to Sartrean and Trotskyist theories of class struggle that informed the early political thought of Félix Guattari. As Andrew Ryder has argued, in these preoccupations with continuing the Bolshevik breakthrough in collective subjectivity, or what Deleuze and Guattari call "assemblage," we can detect a through-line of a Marxist commitment to class struggle.

traditional Freudian model), they propose a concept of "nonidentifica-tion" linked to a reading of signs as the means for thinking new forms of solidarity across identity groups. Taking the fact of identity and identifica-tion as a reality, this form of nonidentification places emphasis on identifi-cation with the sign of social repression in lieu of the signifier of the identity group as such. The intention here is to propose a form of solidar-ity based on signs that are in social forms of repression and stoppages to desire. The potential for solidarity thus resides in a new way of reading signs and forming praxis around signs that cut across identities. This way of reading the mysterious forms of repressive investment of signs and iden-tification makes for a valuable theory of group solidarity and Deleuze and Guattari form much of their thought, including the key concept "line of flight" from the black radical tradition and, in particular, the thought of the American black revolutionary George Jackson (Koerner 2011).

While Deleuze and Guattari's critique of Oedipus, and by extension psychoanalysis, is tied to an important political project, with the passage of time and the conditions of social fragmentation brought on under neolib-eralism, the anti-Oedipal critique, like its accelerationist project that finds so much influence from their thought, needs to be seen as having reached fundamental dead-end in terms of a philosophy of liberation. As Lacan and the Slovene School have argued, Oedipus is a de-normative and de-stabilizing form of subjectivity that does not *necessarily signify a depen-dence upon the father as an authoritarian figure* and nor does Oedipal subjectivity bring the subject to a blind repetition of the Oedipal complex itself. On the contrary, Oedipus is what figures a break from the father's authority in a way that disrupts all traditional roles within the family. As Étienne Balibar argues:

> The family structure is not based on Oedipus, but Oedipus, to the contrary, inscribes the conflict and the variability of subjective positions into its core and thus hinders any possibility for the family to impose the roles which it prescribes as simple functions for individuals to fulfill "normality." (p. 337)

We claim that Oedipus is what de-roots the family and prevents its nor-mal functioning. As Mladen Dolar argues; in Oedipus, every subject is placed into an impasse, and no subject can simply occupy his or her place (p. 23). We thus envision a primary task of emancipatory politics to be one of reconfiguring the superego in an immanent socio-political arrange-ment. In other words, as Lasch hinted, the social superego is driving nihilistic politics and the theoretical task is not to destroy institutions such as the family and to drive an acceleration of capitalist de-territorialization and fragmentation; the task is to develop a different sort of necessity of the family as a revolutionary agency.

To what extent does non-identitarian and Schizoanalytic praxis, which remains some of the most important insights from Deleuze and Guattari's collaboration, presuppose a certain leisure time which is all but suffocated into non-existence in the current neoliberal social order? There is an implicit trap, far different than what they call the "trap of Oedipus," which risks capturing its subjects in a cycle of adolescence—a permanent revolt against an Oedipal dynamic they can't effectively get out of.

In his later years, following his collaboration with Guattari, Deleuze began to question the political efficacy of the anti-Oedipal project as he began to see the concepts of liberation and revolution that he and Guattari had developed begin to hit the wall of ultra-liberalism. In other words, the core method and praxis of *Anti-Oedipus* and the accelerationist politics that underpin these concepts began to face a paradox like the paradox of liberation: de-territorialization and "lines of flight," or strategies for exit that pose a strong break with Oedipus, miss a more embedded Oedipal logic at play within the social arrangement of power. Bernard Stiegler writes, "he [Deleuze] becomes critical of what he and Guattari and opened in *Anti-Oedipus, A Thousand Plateaus,* and many other texts. I think he begins to take a little step back. He has aged, and he perhaps finds a little limited this kind of yes to the capitalist 'desiring machine', which had become more and more an attitude and less and less a thought" (p. 7).

Both Deleuze and Guattari's politics are varied and can arguably be read in distinction to one another. What is striking, however, is the anti-Oedipal critique had hit the wall of ultra-liberalism. This led him to even revise his revolutionary ideas of Oedipus. The de-territorializing praxis of *Anti-Oedipus* now shifted to a different, more immanent, and radical politics that was more in-tune with the importance of a politics of the negative and of determination. Deleuze's later philosophy is political in a different way than the anti-Oedipal period and this shift is evident in Deleuze's influential essay "Postscript on the Societies of Control" (1992).

In this text, Deleuze works from a Marxian theory of power and argues that our society has become a "control society," in distinction to a "disciplinary society" and that power is not to be thought of as "uni-causal" or only tethered to one causal agent such as the proletariat, the class struggle, and so on. Rather, in control societies, which Deleuze sees arising in rudimentary form in the late nineteenth century, power moves away from disciplinary or juridical power to the idea that there are many forms of power, and that society is an "archipelago" of different powers.

Deleuze importantly notes that the idea of power we find in control societies is in concert with Marx's idea of various "meshes of power" and Marx's writings on post-industrial society discuss different forms of power.[3] What is important to note here is that the transition from a disciplinary society to a control society is fundamentally bound up with changes in the division of labor. One of the most important insights Deleuze homes in on in this text is the idea that in the control societies, "institutions come before the state"; that is, institutions possess internal mechanisms of power that are no longer reliant on centralized states:

> The conquests of the market are made by grabbing control and no longer by disciplinary training, by fixing the exchange rate much more than by lowering costs, by transformation of the product more than by specialization of production. Corruption thereby gains a new power. Marketing has become the center or the "soul" of the corporation. We are taught that corporations have a soul, which is the most terrifying news in the world. The operation of markets is now the instrument of social control and forms the impudent breed of our masters. Control is short-term and of rapid rates of turnover, but also continuous and without limit, while discipline was of long duration, infinite and discontinuous. (p. 6)

The mechanism of power is horizontally distributed across institutions and thus the very efficacy of power is maintained by a certain superegoic function, although Deleuze does not frame it this way precisely. To incorporate our concept of the social superego, we can understand the shift to control societies as a shift from a model of authority based on the "you must not" (prohibition) to a "you can" (permissive) attitude. This interior shift in power is also to be understood as affecting the composition of the division of labor wherein individuals take it upon themselves to "self-regulate" their performance.

Deleuze's insights into the new forms of power affecting our current social order in the proposal of the "control societies" shed light on why

---

[3] For a careful analysis of how the Foucault-inspired idea of "meshes of power" possesses a common link to Marx's analysis of power, please see Foucault, Michel, "The Mesh of Power," translated by Christopher Chitty September 12, 2012, *Viewpoint* magazine: https://viewpointmag.com/2012/09/12/the-mesh-of-power/

the anti-Oedipal political praxis seemed to fail: the interior mechanism of psychic and regulative control mechanisms have become so interiorized to subjective life and so tied up with institutions and social reproduction that they re-produce "metastable" institutions that are flexible, even impervious to destruction, as we find in the guiding ethos of Silicon Valley. The control societies are immune to exaggerated lines of flight; they render the very project of "escape" as superfluous, and the anti-Oedipal critique has even been co-opted by fascistic and reactionary currents of thought that pervert the ideas of capitalist de-territorialization toward supporting extreme libertarian capitalism.

References

Balibar, É. (1997). *La crainte des masses* (p. 337). Galilée.

Deleuze, G. (1992). Postscript on the Societies of Control. *October, 59*(Winter), 3–7.

Deleuze, G., & Guattari, F. (2009). *Anti-Oedipus: Capitalism and Schizophrenia* (R. Hurley, Trans.). Penguin Books.

Dolar, M. (2008). Freud and the Political. *Unbound, 4*(15), 23.

Foucault, M. (2012, September 12). The Mesh of Power (C. Chitty, Trans.), *Viewpoint Magazine*. https://viewpointmag.com/2012/09/12/the-mesh-of-power/

Girard, R. (1978). *"To double business bound": Essays on Literature, Mimesis, and Anthropology* (pp. 84–120). The Johns Hopkins University Press.

Koerner, M. (2011). Line of Escape: Gilles Deleuze's Encounter with George Jackson. *GEN, 44*(2), 157–180.

Reich, W. (1980). *The Mass Psychology of Fascism* (V. Carfagno, Trans.). Farrar, Straus and Giroux.

Ryder, A. (2019, August 17). 'The Function of Autonomy': Félix Guattari and New Revolutionary Prospects. *Salvage Magazine*. https://salvage.zone/online-exclusive/the-function-of-autonomy-felix-guattari-and-new-revolutionary-prospects/

Stiegler, B. (2015). We Have to Become the Quasi-cause of Nothing – Of Nihil. An Interview with Bernard Stiegler. Interview by Judith Wambacq and Bart Buseyne (D. Ross, Trans. and Introduction). See https://biblio.ugent.be/publication/7253001/file/8044558.pdf

CHAPTER 8

Liberalism and the Oedipal

Abstract This chapter argues that liberal theories of the subject and liberal theories of the promotion of equality and justice perpetuate an Oedipal problem. We consider two preeminent liberal thinkers—Ralph Waldo Emerson and John Rawls, and locate a similar paternalistic reliance on submission to untranscendable political authority in both thinkers. We argue that Rawls and Emerson are emblematic of a wider liberal Oedipal problem that creates conditions that foment resentment, rivalry, and anti-solidarity.

Keywords John Rawls • Ralph Waldo Emerson • Meritocracy • Paternalism • Liberal Oedipal problem • Submission • Liberalism

Although Deleuze's (1992) control societies essay provides a very useful historical account of the wider constellation of power that has enveloped our present epoch, it does not get at the core of the *subjective basis of power* that is bound up with the liberal order. For a political order that prides itself on freedom of speech and expression and on toleration of difference, liberalism must also be understood as founded on a series of highly contradictory principles and commitments that fundamentally make liberalism an antagonist to the realization of egalitarian principles (Losurdo, 2014). Rarely is liberalism confronted on terms other than what it sets for

© The Author(s), under exclusive license to Springer Nature
Switzerland AG 2022
D. Tutt, *Psychoanalysis and the Politics of the Family: The Crisis of
Initiation*, The Palgrave Lacan Series,
https://doi.org/10.1007/978-3-030-94070-6_8

itself. Most often, liberal thought is treated with a certain realism; we can even propose an inverse of what Mark Fisher calls "capitalist realism" and speak of *liberal realism*. Liberalism is the air that we breathe. Yet despite this disciplined realism we face with liberalism, it is important to note that since the fall of "really existing socialism" in 1990, the liberal order has faced several crises of legitimacy that have exposed its complicity with a system of global market capitalism[1]—with that a tacit support for the preservation of a status quo of extreme inequalities.

Liberal thought—and *liberalists* for that matter—have, since the birth of liberalism in Europe in the sixteenth century, "[tended to be] subjective and anarchist, to be eager for the change which comes from individual initiative, to be insistent that this initiative contains within itself some necessary seed of social good" (p. 16). In the historian Harold Laski's (1997) analysis of the *longue durée* of liberalism, he notices how liberalism tends to make an antithesis between liberty and equality, seeing in liberty the means for individual action for which it is always zealous, and in equality, liberalism tends to see an authoritarian intervention which cramps individual personality (p. 17). The authoritarian impulse implicit in liberalism, which we mentioned above, emerges from its early historical foundation as a political doctrine meant to defend the property rights of the emerging bourgeois class in the seventeenth century.

As a result of its triumphant status in our world today, liberalism is rarely thought of as offering up a theory of the subject, that is, as presenting a comprehensive solution, on its own terms, to the problem of subjectivity. But liberalism does have a theory of the subject that informs and shapes its idea of citizenship and of the subject's relation to social power. Despite its origin in a break from tyrannous confessional authority structurers in the medieval church, liberalism is not an impartial political doctrine open to a multitude of subjective expressions.

In this chapter, we intend to argue liberalism also possess disciplinary tendencies, and that as a system of political and social thought, it has a long history of maintaining implicit support for imperialism, capitalism, and even slavery in the nineteenth century and before (2014). Our thesis,

---

[1] There is a cottage industry of books following the defeat of Hillary Clinton in 2016 to Donald Trump which examines the decline of liberalism and the concomitant decline in trust in liberal elites. In this chapter we are more interested in examining the liberal tendencies toward subjectivity, that is, in the ways that liberal theories of self-agency and social power inform and give cover to the more anti-egalitarian form of liberalism which thinkers like Domenico Losurdo (2014) write very presciently about.

in what follows, is that liberalism also has an Oedipal problem that it can't resolve, and this is found in its theory of citizenship and in the very underpinnings of liberal ideals of egalitarianism and justice.[2] Liberalism's Oedipal problem is an *unthought* problem and we find it in two of the most preeminent liberal philosophers: Ralph Waldo Emerson and John Rawls. Emerson's thought articulates a comprehensive spiritual and cosmic account of the subject rooted and submitted to liberal social and political conditions. In Rawls' liberal theory of "justice as fairness," we are presented with a form of egalitarianism that relies, like Emerson's, on a parental model of submission.

While this chapter is not the place for a comprehensive critique of liberal political thought and its treatment of psychic authority and submission, there are several works that have addressed this topic.[3] We aim to show how two of the most central liberal thinkers present a theory of subjective freedom that remains stuck with irresolvable Oedipal problems. One could argue that from a more general, or even structural sense, liberalism relies on Oedipal authority due to its pseudo-anarchist tendencies which have been with liberalism since its founding and expressed in the ways that liberalism privileges individual liberty as a tonic to equality. This privileging of liberty *naturalizes forms of market domination* as merely par for the course, that is, as an inevitable condition of social life which is then given the ideological name of "liberty." Liberalism thus packages a major part of subjective freedom in a negative ideal of liberty. Socialist critiques of liberal thought typically argue that to truly achieve the promises of egalitarian social relations, the reliance on an unchecked market sphere forecloses any such prospect (Honneth 2016).[4]

---

[2] We are theorizing liberalism's theory of citizenship as analogous to its wider theory of the subject, both of which are political and far from merely "neutral" theories that make space for a multitude of different gender, racial or religious subjective expressions. We maintain that liberalism does give ground to identities and difference while it also portends a political adherence to figures of paternal authority.

[3] There are several psychoanalytic critiques of liberalism from the early 2000s by Slavoj Žižek which diagnose "liberal tolerance" and its ideological functions, and the work of Joan Copjec stands out here as well, and her essay on Rawls and envy is discussed below.

[4] There is a well-established critique of liberalism often given by socialists such as Axel Honneth, who argues that to achieve the sort of equality within the economic sphere that liberalism proclaims, we insist that the economic sphere which liberalism arrogates to the market be treated with forms of "social freedom" that the spheres of civil society and the nation are granted to liberal subjects. Honneth proposes a praxis of solidarity that might "offer a mechanism or scheme of action according to which the freedom of each would

In Emerson, the stakes of submission to the market are elevated beyond mere pragmatic ideals of liberty. The American bard develops a wider theory of the individual that perfects liberal power by conditioning the subject to laws which they cannot change, that is, submission to Oedipal adherence the subject cannot modify. This reading of Emerson's political thought is owed in large part to *The Emerson Effect: Individualism and Submission in America* (1996), a groundbreaking work of revisionist historical interpretation on Emerson by Christopher Newfield.

Although the Transcendentalist movement that Emerson gave birth to in the late nineteenth century is known to champion values of self-reliance and possessive individualism, and at times progressive support for social issues such as the ending of slavery, Newfield shows that Emerson's liberalism was far more aristocratic. Emerson gets rid of possessive individualism and replaces that with a common helplessness and stresses the importance of cultivating an indifference to the strength of others. This means that power does not lead to domination but to an always changing equalization, and by extension, the citizen (or subject) must submit to a "flexible but unchanging higher law" (p. 43).

If submission to the right law is properly met, then equality becomes irrelevant in Emerson's system of thought. Newfield convincingly shows how Emerson develops the framework for an enduring corporate notion of individualism that, "consists of obeying a massive (yet benevolent) administrative power which is private and out of one's control" (p. 63). This benevolent administrative power becomes the source of resolution, and in a telling passage Emerson writes of self-reliance and notes that achieving "it was not [based on] oneself or my immediate democratic community. It was still *the father, my fate, "demetaphysicalized" into the sameness of pumpkins*" (p. 34). What Newfield's analysis points out is a dep paternalism at the heart of Emerson's theory of liberal subjectivity.

For Emerson, power does not lead to domination but to an always changing equalization, and this is not the equalization of a more autonomous agency but the release and forfeiting of it on behalf of each subject. We can thus read Emerson through Newfield's project, into our own and show that Emerson, as a great liberal philosopher proposes a version of Oedipal authority that relies on "submission to a flexible but unchanging higher law" (p. 34).

directly presuppose the freedom of the other"—see Honneth, Axel *The Idea of Socialism: Towards a Renewal*, Polity Press, Malden, MA, 2016, 77.

Submission to the right law, which is unchangeable for the subject, makes equality irrelevant and Emerson develops a corporate notion of individualism that assumes the possibility of a public, collective agency which would reflect group sovereignty based on this submission. The problem with this form of obedience to Oedipal authority is that it negatively affects political action and forges dynamics in which subjects are tethered to Oedipal authority they can't question or transcend. It is in this way that we find in Emerson the propensity to expand Oedipal logics of paternal reliance on authority in such a way that they are transferred to institutions as such. But the problem with this transfer process is that those dynamics are not permitted to work-through their reliance on authority but must instead come to accept them.

It is for this reason that the Emersonian view of liberal equality is similar to what Lasch (1976) calls a "repressive egalitarianism" and which is at the core of the production of *resentment*. This resentment stems from the fact that it is an equality that does not effectively resolve the Oedipal problem because it presents Oedipal authority as untranscendable. Sibling rivalry becomes transposed onto the wider network of institutions; it escapes the confines of the family:

> It is precisely the experience of competing for parental favors with his rival siblings that prepares the American child to live in the society he will enter as an adult—a society in which most of the avenues of achievement (such as they were) have been closed off and in which he will once again have to compete with his peers for the favors dispensed by those in power. (p. 14)

In effect, the Oedipal problem of liberal political thought makes power out to be "pre-Oedipal"; that is, power is based on adhering to its prerequisites. Power is not based on an Oedipal model in which power is accepted, worked-through and transcended.

In Chap. 5, "Oedipus: A Function of Initiation," we aimed to articulate how a Oedipus can be furthered in social arrangements such that the very problem of Oedipal dynamics can be worked-through and power and authority can be accepted and then transcended. We also showed how Oedipus is a theory of subjective de-normalization; that is, it is a drama about the working-through of reliance on Oedipal power. In Emerson's theory of power, the liberal subject does not desire to replace the existing powers, it only aims to *negotiate with them for new privileges and favors*. This aim to negotiate with power, but not to work-through and truly contest and transform power marks liberalism and all its wide spectrum of expression, to ultra-liberalism to conservative variants of liberalism. Put differently, the tendency to treat power as pre-Oedipal means those in power—the ruling class, the elite, bosses, and so on—are effectively untouchables and their authority, and even their position, is untranscendable.

Liberalism has a long history of treating power in a pre-Oedipal fashion. Consider the historian Louis Hartz's highly influential argument in *The Liberal Tradition in America* (1955), that the American Revolution, because it was a bourgeois revolution—primarily conceived in demands for greater market freedoms for the bourgeois class—was marked by the absence of feudal social relations. Hartz (1991) convincingly argues the American Revolution was a solidly bourgeois revolution unlike the French Revolution and other European revolutions of the early nineteenth century which overthrew the ruling class, specifically the aristocracy. The absence of feudalism in the American context meant that the revolution never killed the primal father of the British crown, King George III, and nor did the American revolutionaries truly conceive of the revolution as an overthrow of the class system.

This inability to kill the primal father created a dynamic that Hartz calls an "inverted Freudianism" where no primal father was ever killed. The Americans, unlike the French, did not kill their king, but eventually over the course of the revolution effigies of King George were burned, but this was only much later in the sequence of the revolution. Hartz goes on to argue that the inverted Freudianism of the American Revolutionaries resulted in a *terminal liberalism* which has historically treated antagonisms such as class struggle and the rise of pernicious inequalities, slavery, and racial oppressions to all be treated by liberal solutions which maintain the power of the bourgeois class.

For Hartz, the metaphysical sameness of all that Emerson envisioned as the basis of social freedom was akin to what he called "metaphysical Lockeanism," a tendency that has prevented any true contestation to America's liberal tradition. American political thought has a pre-Oedipal problem in the very way political dynamics are embedded in American politics, and this has meant that "no comfortable aristocracy awaited the millionaire success and no apocalyptic dream of revolution functioned as solace for the failed proletariat" (p. 211).

By the late nineteenth-century "Gilded Age" and Reconstructionist period, at the early dawn of the racial system known as "Jim Crow," Hartz pinpoints the emergence of a particular liberal ideology that emerged to conceal the class struggle and antagonisms that come from capitalist inequalities in what he calls "Algerism." This ideology presents a competitive solution for working classes and racialized subjects in America, promising them an escape of their conditions through cultivating a meritocratic grit and entrepreneurial work ethic (pp. 62–63).

Modelled off the best-selling novels of Horatio Alger, which tell mythical stories of poor young orphans who rise out of the working class through the *paternalistic support of a rich benefactor* by hard work and determination, "Algerism" became the primary enforcement ideology and primary means to quell class struggle. Hartz tracks the consistency of the "Alger mythos" from the Gilded Age of the late nineteenth century on through to the New Deal period, which was primarily permitted by the ruling class because it delivered the single largest expansion of private property in history. The Alger-meritocratic-mythos has been the biggest single deterrent to the emergence of a socialistic alternative in American history:

> The word of Alger excluded the word of Marx in America. So long as the American millionaire stood at the apex of the Alger scheme he did not symbolize the fulfillment of the Marxian hope. (p. 253)

American liberalism, and arguably liberalism stretching back to its European roots in the sixteenth century, has an Oedipal problem. In the American context, this Oedipal problem revolves around a necessary reliance on paternalistic authority that has prevented the emergence of socialist challenges to liberal hegemony and these dynamics often pervert any attempt to change the status quo. The liberal Oedipal problem is not merely a relic of America's bourgeois revolutionary past but lives on in the paternalistic structure of its ideological glue: Algerism and its more contemporary avatar "meritocracy."

Now that we have a more historical footing to the paternalistic basis of America's history of meritocracy, it's a convenient time to introduce John Rawls, the most influential philosopher of liberal meritocracy. Rawlsian thought is steeped in a commitment to furthering a society built on meritocratic competition and his political thought can be understood of furthering an ideological continuation Algerism. Although Rawls presents his arguments in *A Theory of Justice* (1971) as opposed to meritocracy, arguing for fairness of opportunity in the need for fairness in competitions for social positions and offices, we will argue that he ends up supporting much the same liberal paternalistic forms of subjective submission that we find in Emerson.

Rawlsianism is not distinct to America, although the "asset-owning" post welfare state policies of Bill Clinton in the early 1990s were deeply influenced by Rawlsian meritocratic ideals (Milanović 2019). In *Capitalism, Alone* (2019), the American economist Branko Milanović identifies the two dominant forms of contemporary capitalism: the authoritarian directed capitalism of China and "liberal meritocratic capitalism" for which the latter is fundamentally shaped by Rawlsian ideas of equality. At the basic level of Rawls' theory of equality, he places no legal constraints to people achieving the same position in life. At this level, Rawls' "first principle of justice" maintains that everyone has the same political liberty regardless of economic or social class. The first principle of justice makes up the basis of Rawls' system of "natural liberty," which is synonymous with "meritocratic capitalism."

Before he became a graduate student in philosophy, Rawls intended to become an Episcopalian priest. His PhD dissertation was on the political theology of Pelagianism, a fourth-century Christian heretic who preached against a natural conception of original sin and who embraced a doctrine of the fundamental goodness of the human being. Eric Nelson (2019) has written about how Rawls developed a sophisticated notion of "luck egalitarianism" in opposition to the legacy of Pelagian theories of more strict egalitarianism. In Rawls' second principle of justice, "equality of opportunity" a series of correctives must be applied to natural and socially derived inequalities such as to what family one is born, what genetics one inherits and so on.

In his magnum opus, *A Theory of Justice* (1971) Rawls discusses Freud, and by extension psychoanalysis, in three areas of the text. In each mention of Freud, Rawls does not shy from painting Freud's Oedipal theory as "non-rational." Rawls is dismissive of Freud, claiming that the theory of the superego indicates that moral learning for children is typically "irrational and without justification." Freud's insights are treated by Rawls as something to do away with in the act of consent to the original position, and he thus conveys a desire to do away with the psychoanalytic insights into the moral situation of humankind, even though he wrestles with and considers Freud's insights at various places in *A Theory of Justice*.

In Rawls' discussion of Freud in the section on "envy and justice" he aims to arrive at a definitive idea of the "natural condition" of the human and how these conditions can best satisfy the principles of justice and agree to the original position. In a very cursory reading of Freud's *Group Psychology and the Analysis of the Ego* (1921) Rawls claims Freud treats envy as the constitutive basis of human relations that is converted in a "reaction formation" in which the members of society agree to set envy down through a pact or social contract from which justice can then flourish. This account of envy and equality is a generally accurate account of Freud's position on the matter, but as Joan Copjec has pointed out, Rawls misses the deeper logic that envy plays in Freudian thought. It is not that envy emerges based on a desire for the object of another's desire; "the affect of envy is not a matter of desire or an appeal to others for recognition, but of jouissance, which seeks no such validation" (p. 164).

Copjec shows how Rawls mistakes the cause of envy in the other and this is evident in his discussion of sibling rivalry, where he argues that the jealousy of one sibling feels upon witnessing the other receive breast milk is based on the worry that the source of the milk will dry out and be unavailable. In other words, Rawls (1971) argues the envious feeling in sibling rivalry is brought on by envy of the other's object (p. 539). In the Freudian view, envy is rather brought about by the other's satisfaction, as Copjec (2003) maintains "envy envies satisfaction, enjoyment" (p. 540).

Rawls insists from the outset of his discussion of envy and justice that "a rational individual is not subject to envy" and his theory assumes "the absence of envy and a lack of knowledge of the special psychologies." (p. 530). He differentiates between general and particular envy: the former, "general envy" is experienced by those least advantaged, and it happens when envy the advantaged for the goods they have access to, not the specific objects they possess. "Particular envy" is experienced as rivalry over objects that typically has to do with relations in which one loses out on a job or loses out to another in a competition for acquiring a particular position. But whether it is the specific object of envy—the coveted job, for example—or the object of the more advantaged goods, in both instances, envy is thought to emerge from desiring the other's objects of desire.

The problem with Rawls' theory of envy is that he forecloses the problem of envy entirely, relegating "strict egalitarianism" to inevitably producing envy as the *cause* of equality. In other words, in his theory of justice envy is not treated as a constitutive basis of the agreement of the various principles of justice. In his interpretation of the nursery example of sibling rivalry, he argues that envy emerges from "the attention and affection of their parents, to which ... they justly have an equal claim" (p. 540). In the example of sibling rivalry envious demands are "bids for recognition from a *parental other deemed capable of granting it.*" As Copjec rightly points out, such bids are precisely what Freud's theory of the envious origins of the demand for equality have prepared us to expect and as such, any political theory of justice must take envy into account for more directly than Rawls is willing to (Copjec, 2003, 166).

Curiously, resentment is a "moral feeling" in Rawls' estimation; he argues resentment typically calls forth a reason for its feelings of spite. When we resent others, it typically has to do with unjust institutions or to a particular social problem, whereas envy is treated by Rawls as a vice, a taboo quasi-theological conundrum. This is different than envy, which is not a moral feeling but a vice that has to be discarded in the same way that an Aristotelian virtue theorist would discard a sinful emotion or affect.

Rawls correctly recognizes the danger inherent in envy—its tendency to lead to unhinged rancor and even situations that perpetuate social violence—but in his steadfast abhorrence of taking the problem of envy seriously as a problem of enjoyment and satisfaction as such, Rawls rejects any psychological theory of envy that might disturb what he is aiming at in the original position. He will suggest that "strict egalitarianism," which insists on the equal distribution of goods equally among the members of society produces envy, whereas Rawls' "luck egalitarianism" does not face the problem of envy because in the original position, "no one is moved by rancor or spite." The acceptance of the two principles of justice and of equality more generally would take place on the presupposition that "envy does not exist."

Where Rawls links up with Emerson and where both theorists fall sway to the liberal Oedipal problem resides in the role of parental recognition and parental submission that is placed in an untranscendable position in both accounts. Rawls' theory of justice perpetuates social relations which cannot transcend structures of envy because the basis of the achievement of justice is forged in relation to a "mean" of pleasure and happiness. Importantly, the principle of justice is not based on an axiom or on an ideal, it is rather a principle that must be realized based on conditions that are immanent to the social order itself. The difference between jealousy and envy is crucial here; in jealousy I simply want what the other has and I vie for attaining it through competition to acquire the coveted object.

In envy, I don't exactly aim to acquire the object but rather seek to block the other's possibility of ever attaining the object. Envy is a far more frustrated affect, and as the philosopher and as Copjec (2003) has argued, it is Rawls' theory of envy (that is found in his critique of Freud) that reproduces reliance on a paternalistic authority source for recognition and this dynamic perpetuates the liberal Oedipal problem:

> What corrals his [Rawls'] theory, maintaining it within the expanded field of utilitarianism, is his commitment to normative judgment, to a measure or standard of pleasure, which is the inevitable consequence of his insistence on "parental" recognition. Ignorant of the structure of pleasure—which, as Freud taught, is only ever partial, never complete—and believing naively that complete satisfaction is attainable by anyone who, unimpeded by bad fortune, sets about realizing a rational plan, Rawls is not well positioned to see that the need for recognition of one's desire is also the occasion of envy. (pp. 167–168)

If a theory of equality and justice is founded on a *median* of an ideal that is determined by capitalist forms of market exchange, this results in the perpetuation of envious social relations that produce squabbles and conflicts that are incapable of usurping the very median itself. Liberal political thought cannot touch the other, or the site of authority that determines the mean of pleasure. What this means is that liberalism derives its theory of equality as hyper-immanent to the very capitalist order itself, leaving untouched the domination of market relations and keeping paternal authority structures in place as nodes of necessary recognition. The immanence of liberalism offers no reprieve or cover from market domination. In fact, liberalism is often most true to its form, most honest with its tendencies, when it sees itself from its more extreme right-wing variations, that is, as libertarian and insistent that market domination is not domination, but freedom. Even the more moderate liberal philosophies of Emerson and Rawls cannot escape this limited framework of social freedom that is reliant on domination and submission.

REFERENCES

Copjec, J. (2003). *Imagine There Is No Woman: Ethics and Sublimation*. MIT Press.

Deleuze, G. (1992). Postscript on the societies of control. *October, 59*(winter), 3–7.

Hartz, L. (1991). *The Liberal Tradition in America*. Harcourt, Inc.

Honneth, A. (2016). *The Idea of Socialism: Towards a Renewal*. Polity Press.

Lasch, C. (1976). *The Family as a Haven in a Heartless World*. Salmagundi, Skidmore College (No. 35, pp. 42–55. 14).

Laski, H. (1997). *The Rise of European Liberalism*. Transaction Publishers.

Losurdo, D. (2014). *Liberalism: A Counter-History* (G. Elliott, Trans.). Verso Books.

Milanović, Branko (2019). *Capitalism, Alone: The Future of the System that Rules the World*. Harvard University Press.

Nelson, E. (2019). *The Theology of Liberalism: Political Philosophy and the Justice of God*. Harvard University Press.

Newfield, C. (1996). *Emerson Effect*. University of Chicago Press.

Rawls, J. (1971). *A Theory of Justice*. Harvard University Press.

CHAPTER 9

The Political Stakes of the Social Superego

Abstract This chapter discusses the idea of the political and the origin, or "birth" of the political in psychoanalytic theory, by considering Freud's theory of the primal father from *Totem and Taboo*. We argue that Freud theorized a distinct "non-subject" at the origin of any emergence of political change and thus of a re-composition of the superego. We then analyze what sort of non-subjects are important figures to think about today. We conclude this chapter with a consideration from popular culture that exemplifies the emergence of the political and a break with the social superego: Todd Philip's 2018 film *Joker* with Joaquin Phoenix.

Keywords Social superego • Non-subject • Joker • Primal father • Origin of the political • *Lumpenproletariat*

We began this book with an examination of how the era of neoliberal capitalism (1973–present) has exhausted the superego rooted in the transmission of ego ideals of the family. We then argued these dynamics have given rise to a "social superego" that does not operate on a function of binding and release from figures of authority, and that it stunts subjects' capacities to more adequately *work-through* that binding and promote autonomy and release. This process leads to the crisis of initiation. The social superego intensifies the process of binding to authority and gives way to the

D. Tutt, *Psychoanalysis and the Politics of the Family: The Crisis of Initiation*, The Palgrave Lacan Series,
https://doi.org/10.1007/978-3-030-94070-6_9

"Oedipal problem" we diagnosed at the very core of the liberal social order. We then demonstrated the Oedipal problem has a historical, and not merely a more recent neoliberal origin, by looking at how the very core of liberal thought retains Oedipal submission in its theory of the subject, and we pinpointed these commitments in Emerson and Rawls.

The Alger mythos is breaking down today, and as it loses its efficacy, the neoliberal order has moved to a new stage of enforcement, a more reactionary stage that William Davies (2016) calls "punitive neoliberalism" (p. 129). Neoliberalism was founded in its earliest iteration in the 1970s as an explicitly political contestation between the ruling class against socialist and labor union power; therefore, neoliberalism must be understood as a political movement that successfully enacted a series of policy overhauls that aimed to elevate the market as the primary vector of self-making and self-discipline. But this dream was not normalized until 1989, and the rise of the policy victory of the neoliberal order soon began to sediment into the fabric of social life throughout the 1990s. What Davies points out is the way the early period of neoliberalism from 1979 to 1989 was a period marked by a "combative" and explicitly political and anti-socialist form of politics.

The post-2008 period of neoliberalism, following the global recession, gave rise to a new stage of "punitive neoliberalism" in which "the 'enemies' targeted now are largely disempowered and internal to the neoliberal system itself. In some instances, such as those crippled by poverty, debt and collapsing social-safety nets, they have already been largely destroyed as an autonomous political force. Yet somehow this increases the urge to punish them further" (p. 132). In the context of this punitive phase of neoliberalism, the political repercussions for the possibility of transforming the status quo within liberalism remain very strained.

We have argued one way to understand the durability of the status quo today is to understand the Oedipal problem at the heart of liberalism, a dynamic which remains part and parcel of liberalism, whether it is in a combative or punitive stage as it is now, or whether it is in a normalized, that is, a relatively crisis-free stage. The Oedipal problem creates several challenges for political liberation: it constrains the work of forgoing solidarities among oppressed groups and classes because it becomes unclear where rivalry starts and where it ends. It creates situations in which it is difficult to rationally diagnose political antagonisms that affect us in common because it narrows antagonisms to an individual imaginary basis of the wounded self.[1]

The liberal Oedipal dynamic intensifies imaginary aggressions, which often lead to exaggerated group behavior, from victim-blaming to censorial and repressive politics.[2] The liberal Oedipal problem also creates a *nominalism out of social antagonisms*; that is, political antagonisms seem to possess a fictional status because they are often tied into unresolved parental dynamics, and these unresolved Oedipal problems haunt actual and real political challenges in the real world. This is not to say, in a cynical way, that liberalism produces "daddy issues" in its subjects because, as we saw in Chap. 3, the social superego tends to make the maternal into the cruel and persecutory force, not the father. But this is merely a tendency, and we are not suggesting that political antagonisms lean more toward the mother or the father in their ambivalences and aggressive identifications.

We are suggesting that there is a general tendency for subjects to struggle to work-through parental dynamics, which is not necessarily the fault of the family, but should be understood as the result of the socialized family adopted by and enshrined in institutions. The family merely becomes the elementary model for the Oedipal structure that is transferred to institutions, and by Oedipal we mean that institutions, from wage labor jobs to colleges, forge relations of familial dependence and require submission to all sorts of hierarchies of order that reflect the family order:

> The workplace, along with prisons and schools, is among history's last remaining universal authoritarian institutions. Absolute monarchies, aristocracies, chattel slavery, fascism, military juntas, and Stalinism have mostly gone. To be sure, many dictatorships remain despite resistance and rebellion,

---

[1] The increase in the trope of the "wounded self" abounds in the wider culture and curiously enough, this is a trope that Lasch identifies as an outgrowth of *The Culture of Narcissism* (1979); that is, there is a tendency to perceive oneself not merely as a victim, for which there are any number of very valid sorts of victims. The dynamic we are talking about is one in which a culture emerges in which people feel that their victimhood is incommensurate and that it cannot be adequately processed by others. We do not offer a critique of "cancel culture" here but we hope that the wider liberal Oedipal problem offers some conceptual tools for understanding it.

[2] For a more historical genealogy of liberal-nominalist versus socialist-realist political epistemologies, see Losurdo, Domenico (1996) "Realism and Nominalism as Political Categories" published in Presses Universitaires de France, Revue de Métaphysique et de Morale, Avril–Juin 1996, 101e Année, No. 2, Philosophie Politique (Avril–Juin 1996), pp. 211–223.

forms of forced labor and human trafficking affect many parts of the world, including the United States, and the return of a slightly modernized fascism is a real danger, "whether reflected in the person of a Marine Le Pen or a Donald Trump. But the workplace or "the job" remains the site of authoritarian rule across the entire globe regardless of the nature of the national political regime, state of economic development, or place in the global economy. This is because it is the bedrock of capitalism everywhere, as well as that of the remnants of so-called communist bureaucratic economies, which are themselves becoming penetrated by capitalism. (Moody, 2017, pp. 196–197)

The cultivation of the family spirit is transferred to institutions and to the workplace wherein the Oedipal problem haunts our institutional life. In such conditions of a stunted Oedipal situation, these institutions often provide no escape other than through entrepreneurial freedom. The era of punitive neoliberalism—2008 to present—only intensifies these dynamics of complicity with the very mechanisms of punitive discipline. These dynamics of punitive enforcement have lost their efficacy of normalized enforcement and in this way the era of punitive neoliberalism also witnesses the reemergence of the political.

But while the Oedipal problem is not directly solvable, as Lacan knew full well, there are social dynamics that can be established in which its dynamics can be more effectively worked-through. But too often, these dynamics of imaginary aggressivity borne from problematic Oedipal dynamics lead to ultra-nominalism, which is another name for the sort of "ultra-liberalism" that Deleuze saw his anti-Oedipal philosophy falling sway to. If political antagonisms are prone to being misplaced and displaced in common institutional life such that they mirror a strained Oedipal dynamic of the family, then personalized aggressions become the common form of political exchange in political discourse. This leads to dynamics within liberal political culture to where even anarchist energies of revolt and insurrection tend to secretly submit to this problematic. In a system dominated by the liberal Oedipal problematic, arrangements of hierarchy and status quo relations are often kept in place even after acting out against authority occurs. But our era is marked by the resurgence of the political and with that resurgence we see new figures of contestation, new movements of solidarity and class struggle are emerging that aim to contest the social order.

In our proposal of the paradox of liberation, we examined how liberationist social change was at the very heart of Freud's discovery of the superego. Moreover, we showed how Freud invented the superego as a political concept meant to maintain this binding and release from authority in the face of liberationist social change all around him. We consider the paradox of liberation not an anti-liberationist insight but a sobering insight that should be further studied and incorporated within emancipatory political movements.[3] We then pinpointed how a crisis of initiation emerges in these conditions and we examined how initiation becomes a crucial subjective and collective problem that is taken up through the turn to tradition, to obscurantic politics and to a more general sense of political and subjective disorientation.

As we saw in our analysis of the superego based around the insights of Karatani and Balibar: the superego is a historically contingent and localized phenomenon. For Karatani, the superego emerges in distinct and local situations of political contestation of the social order; that is, there are periods of capitalist life in which the capitalist order satiates the superego and there are other moments in which crisis—war, revolution, and uprising—gives rise to a new configuration of the superego. In this concluding chapter, we take up this more historical and localized proposal of the superego to think through what a breakdown and rupture of the social superego might entail. We recognize that such a thinking necessitates a thinking-through the paradox of liberation and it invites us to taxonomize, as it were, existing figures of the superego in our political situation. Bernard Stiegler argues that thinking a break from the superego and its already fragmented—or highly socialized—status can only occur by a *rebuilding of the superego*.

Stiegler taps into the same insight we have developed apropos the social superego, namely, that its effects are accelerated by the forces of consumer capitalism, an apparatus that destroys the superego. In Stiegler's (2014) view, psychoanalysis has been unable to think the loss of the superego politically, and this loss portends the stunting of sublimation and the erasure of desire:

> As libidinal energy, desire is produced by that apparatus that transforms the drives into investments in objects, via binding systems that are at once

---

[3] We examine some strategies for incorporating this insight into political cultures on the left in the conclusion to this book.

super-egoic and sublimatory (and these cannot be separated: there is no superego without figures with whom to identify, without those identificatory figures produced by sublimation – the question being to know whether the reverse is also true). (p. 156)

In a similar way to Lasch, Stiegler suggests that a return to a more stable social situation is necessary for desire and sublimation to enact a transformation of subjectivity, that is, to invent a new desire. This loss imposes limitations on subjectivity, limiting what sorts of transformations it can undergo. It also results in a social order where pure drives of destruction and fragmentation are more unruly and prominent. For Stiegler, as we saw for Karatani, a social order that has destroyed superego will face acephalous chaos and subjective violence.

We already saw that Freud's core concepts, from the Oedipus complex to the superego, contain a political principle that animates them. For Lacan's return to Freud, as Samo Tomšič (2013) brilliantly points out, became more explicitly political in his "second return to Freud" which occurred around the time of Lacan's turn to Marx and Marx's theory of production in the late 1960s. Lacan will frequently credit Marx with "inventing the symptom," an insight which extends far beyond the theory of the capitalist discourse, which we explored in Chap. 5. Lacan will affirm that the "unconscious is politics" and in this statement we see him shift away from the structuralist period of his thought in which the "unconscious is structured like a language" (p. 22).

If the unconscious is politics, it is neither an ontological nor a positive entity; it is rather marked by the absence of time and the absence of contradiction and dependent on the actually existing social conditions and ruling ideologies (p. 85). This insight helps us better understand why for Freud, something of the older aristocratic order had to be maintained in the transition from the collapse of the social order upon the conclusion of World War I. Freud was aiming for a neutralization of the political, and thus for him, politics must function as a neutralizing and stabilizing principle for subjectivity. A major challenge to political thinking in our current conjecture revolves around the fact that thinking the movement beyond the extremes of delirium that a political break promises, as we critiqued in Deleuze and Guattari, tends to only affirm the paradox of liberation and to pose only *partial* liberation. Liberation is only partial because one it adheres its liberatory demands to the market those demands are effectively chewed up by the market's logic, not its own.

But the question remains how do we think a break or a rupture with the social superego? Any question of collective emancipation today must begin with a consideration of what in Chap. 5 we referred to as those "without initiation," or what we will more broadly name "non-subjects." In what follows, we aim to examine the central role these figures are given in psychoanalytic thought when it comes to any revolution of, or transformation of a given political situation.

Typically, we imagine the activation and empowerment of non-subjects to spark a more abyssal and violent form of freedom unmoored from any collective solidarity and spontaneously forming in revolt or uprising. And this is accurate: non-subjects can be identified in figures of our present, from the *lumpenproletariat,* to subjects without support or family networks, the homeless, to elements of the transgender rights movement, to racialized "surplus" populations in inner cities that drive uprisings and contestations, to the opioid addicts in former industrial towns across America.[4] These thrown and contingent "non-subjects" are figures of subjective revolution, despite how difficult their non-representational status can be. Non-subjects are interesting to us and tend to pose a profound challenge to liberalism because they *glitch* the neoliberal representation motherboard completely.

Non-subjects are deprived of initiation, and they develop an alternative means for *counter-initiation* through the experience of being thrown to a more random and chance-based life, typically outside of the family. These are forms of subjectivity that exist on the edge of the social entirely, and we can identify some of the predominant forms they take in our world today. The "non-meritorious body", which we discussed in our conversation around Badiou's theory of initiation is one such example of a non-subject because they tend to be deprived of stable work and as a result, they are often deprived of having a family because of precarious living conditions and lack of stable income.

To deny the meritocratic and Alger mythos is itself an act of defiance whether the subject understands their act and their predicament to be political in any form of decision or intention. Another form of the non-subject is found in the black family, and specifically in figures of the working-class black mother, whom Hortense Spillers (1987) identifies as

---

[4] See Clover, Joshua *Riot. Strike. Riot. The New Era of Uprisings* Verso (2016), for an analysis of surplus populations as the vanguard and driving force of contemporary insurrectionary activity and uprisings around the world.

"out of the traditional symbolics of female gender" due to the intense expectations and pressures placed on black single women to take on the role of the father. Black single women are less interested in joining the ranks of gendered femaleness than they are in gaining the "insurgent ground as female social subject" in Spillers' reading (p. 81).

It is important that we not fetishize the non-subject as a negative mode of ideal freedom. The suffering of being deprived a social bond, of being deprived of labor on a stable basis, let alone poorly paid labor, is serious and real. As such, there is an ethical dimension to any discussion of non-subjects and even of the working class and the transformation of the family and politics for these subjectivities. Their very contingent subjectivity can often become secretly envied by academics, theorists and even revolution-aries. It is important to not romanticize the non-subject as a paradoxical ideal of negative freedom. Although the revolutionary Marxist tradition has a long history of working in careful solidarity with "non-subjects," and a long-standing debate in Marxist thought revolves around how to form solidarity with the lumpenproletariat,[5] many contemporary Marxists have veered away from thinking about the lumpenproletariat in the context of theorizing revolution today. The non-subject is analogous to the lumpen-proletariat and this form of subjectivity concerns us given that any re-configuration of the superego must involve non-subjects.

But why is the non-subject at the heart of the reconfiguration of super-ego? To get at this question we must turn to the question of the stakes of "the political" and the ways authority is derived from the political. The philosopher Avital Ronell (2012) points out that psychoanalysis never solves the question that concerned Freud when he wrote *Group Psychology and the Analysis of the Ego*, mainly: "how does authority impose itself upon the group?" (p. 93). The problem of authority is formed around what Ronell calls the "Power-Father"; the emergence of the primal horde explains nothing but the self-organization of the political.

As neoliberalism was in its relatively early political and economic ascen-dancy and the Cold War officially ended in 1990—resulting in the fall of "really existing socialism"—an important, albeit aborted, philosophical

---

[5] In a previous work, I have written on the class composition of the lumpenproletariat today and how solidarity with lumpenproletariat can be thought today. See Tutt, Daniel, "Recentering the Lumpen Question Today: Understanding Lumpenization and Bonapartism," *Spectre* magazine, March 4, 2021 (https://spectrejournal.com/recentering-the-lumpen-question-today)

center arose in France called the *Center for the Philosophical Study of the Political*. It aimed to address the precise status of "the political" in our contemporary world. This important center dedicated itself to a philosophical study of the political and it was convened by prominent French philosophers Jean-Luc Nancy and Phillipe Lacoue-Labarthe (1997). They began with a proposal of the concept of the political as split between two versions of politics: *le politique* and *la politique*. *La politique* is the domain of politics proper, referring to the "maintenance of the Chinese Emperors, the Benin Kings, of Louis XIV, or of German social democracy" (p. 186).

Le Politique, on the other hand, is a "specific dimension of alterity," prior to politics per se but fundamental to its possible modes of articulation or becoming. The political domain is thus a question of relation, more specifically, of relation to that which is prior to politics but linked to social relationality at a fundamental level. Put another way, *le Politique* is the site where what it means to be in common is open for definition, and *la Politique* is the site where different social interests are in conflict over the management and governance of social existence.

Nancy and Lacoue-Labarthe frame the contemporary situation as marked by a "retreat of the political;" they argue, rather bombastically, that the "figure of the human" within the tradition of Western metaphysics is in retreat. They suggest that the entire European philosophical tradition is a continuation of the Christian spread of culture starting with its Greek origins and that this tradition has sought to complete itself in various ways in recent times in the form of liberal democracy, national socialism, and Marxist socialism.

The closure of the political is thus the closure of these big grand political projects. In a way their thesis is reminiscent of Lyotard's idea that postmodernism is the "end of grand narratives." But Nancy and Lacoue-Labarthe interest us because they provide an account of the end of a certain form of the political in our time, but this is an end that *may* be showing signs of reemergence. In our present, totalitarianism or "totality" is an intrinsic part of each of these different figures that sought to master a principle of transcendence; that is, the totalitarian tendency in political ideologies such as National Socialism and state communism is a philosophical problem in that each figures aimed to bring about a certain social totality. In their vision, we lack the very capacity to call upon the same mode of transcendence or alterity today:

The retreat of the political appears first of all as the retreat of transcendence or alterity. Which clearly does not mean that it is for us a matter of repeating the appeal to transcendence, whether it be God, Man, or History: these are the transcendences which have installed totalitarianism or those in which it has installed itself, converting them into the immanence of life-in-common. (p. 193)

Nancy and Lacoue-Labarthe make the political a fundamental philosophical problem and suggest we "must allow or even impose, the tracing of anew the stakes of the political" (p. 194).

What Nancy and Lacoue-Labarthe's argument of the retreat of the political points to is the following dynamic: in the oscillation between these two forms of politics we do not have an immediate collective subjectivity that can be pointed to as a form of consciousness, that is, we lack an identifiable agent of historical change or transformation. This calls forth a politics that is more experimental and creative at the level of subjectivity, it calls forth a thinking of subjective figures of emancipation.

In the conclusion to his masterful work, *The Political Unconscious* (1981), Frederic Jameson points to this same problem and states that a thinking of "the collective" dimension of subjectivity, and a conception of social unity expressed in the "body of the despot" has brought religion back to the table of collective consciousness. This is a similar theme we saw with René Girard; at the end of the grand narratives and the evacuation of the political, religion returns. Jameson recognizes that the problem of collective subjectivity has not been treated in an adequate way, and that until this task is completed, "it seems possible to continue to use a Durkheimian or Lukácsean vocabulary of collective consciousness or of the subject of history "under erasure," provided we understand that any such discussion refers, not to the concepts designated by such terms, but to the as yet untheorized object—the collective—to which they make imperfect allusion" (p. 294).

A social order in which we experience a "retreat of the political," also witnesses the emergence of different figures of its possible rebirth. Alain Badiou (2012a, b) points to a possible "rebirth of history" as found in the uprisings enveloping the world in the "Movement of the Squares" from Egypt to Turkey to New York city in the form of Occupy Wall Street (Badiou, 2012a, b). Although these movements have mostly faced different forms of defeat and state repression, Badiou was right to point to them as a signal of a movement out of what Nancy and Lacoue-Labarthe the retreat of the political. But the fact that these figures of revolt emerged only to effectively disappear points to the persistence of the same oscillation that Nancy and Lacoue-Labarthe claim marks our epoch, namely, the oscillation between politics (ordinary social superego of late capitalism) and the political (the emergence of different collective figures).

How does the function of the infamous primal father play into this interplay of the political? We saw that in the American liberal context, ever since its founding there has been an ambivalence around the killing of the primal father that led Louis Hartz to refer to the American Revolution as "inverted Freudianism." There is a necessary confrontation with and overcoming of the primal father in Freudian thought more broadly. But as Lacan observes in the shift in the authority of the father in the modern period—a shift that was toward a more debased function of the father—this change altered the paternal function and changed the way ego ideals function in the wider society. This change in paternal authority also modified the functioning of the ego ideal, resulting in two possible effects: "'possible political catastrophes' and 'generalized psychopathological effects'" (p. 57).

The "possible political catastrophes" are no longer merely possible, but seem to appear all around us, from the persistence of neofascist movements within the heart of Western European and even within mainstream parliamentary political parties, to structural inequality, and heightened racism. Such a situation of political catastrophe after catastrophe calls for a thinking-through of the *ur*-father who haunts the collective. A social order that cannot work-through authority figures will invent monstrous figures of authority in the face of this impossibility, or it will tend to witness political upheaval after upheaval.

Freud's theory of the primal father in *Totem and Taboo* (1913) is a figure at the origin of any social contract and must be thought and *worked-through* before any thinking of the stakes of the political. The primal father must be thought precisely so that he is overcome and transcended and put to rest. We argue that psychoanalysis does have a theory for treating this conundrum of the primal father, but it comes from outside, it does not come from a figure of authority. Ronell (2012) and Nancy and Lacoue-Labarthe (1997) point out that Freud never derived an analysis of an institution based on such the problematic authority of the primal father. In other words, *psychoanalysis never developed a way to deal with the primal father other than through Oedipus*. Oedipus remains, as Lacan (1947) noted at the immediate conclusion of World War II, "a problem for which, as is well known, a complete solution was never found" (p. 14). By this Lacan meant to suggest that the Oedipal complex poses a problem for group dynamics in general.

In his thinking of the political, Freud did not point out that a benevolent and loving father figure must be at the center of the group's identifications. The solution Freud offers to the problematic of the primal father portends important political ramifications. At the heart of the political Freud identifies a subject that was "neither from other subjects nor from a subject-discourse (whether it be of the other or of the same, of the father or of the brother) but from the *non-subjects*" (p. 6). This non-subject is "without-father" and "without authority"; as Nancy and Lacoue-Labarthe note, the non-subject is "anterior to every topic and institution, an anteriority which no regression can properly catch up, and wider than any founding agency" (p. 6).

The non-subject is rarely represented in film and television in a way that captures the cultural zeitgeist. Todd Phillip's *Joker* (2019) stands out as one such example of a film that tipped off a major cultural conversation on poverty, destitution, depression, and the consequences of the gutting of social services on the overall mental health of people in our society. The film portrays many of the dynamics that concern us: the stunted Oedipal dynamic that results in extremities of violence and the birth of the political out of a collective of lumpenproletariat of social outcasts and rejects; that is, it tells the story of the usurpation of the primal father and the origin of a society where class struggle is elevated as the central antagonism.

One way to form a political and psychoanalytic reading of *Joker* is by looking at the murder of the main character's two father figures: Thomas Wayne and Murray Franklin. Early in the film we learn that Arthur Fleck forms a paternalistic identification with Murray Franklin, a Johnny Carson-esque talk show host. In watching the Murray show in the comfort of his mother's bed, Arthur fantasizes that Murray is a father figure to him; more precisely he fantasizes that Murray calls on him as an audience member and forms a compassionate solidarity with Arthur's absent father at home. Murray thus forms the father of the symbolic for Arthur, and Arthur imitates the fantasy of Murray's show in all its televisual mediation. This imitation helps Arthur to painfully become a stand-up comedian.

The film brilliantly switches in and out of delusion and reality in such a way the viewer is often unsure whether what has happened is a figment of Arthur's delusions or reality. We are also introduced to Arthur's mother, and we learn that she too suffers from delusions, and her primary delusion is formed around the idea of a father figure: Thomas Wayne, her former employer. Her delusion is that Wayne impregnated her, and that Arthur's true father is Wayne himself. Arthur immediately forms a childish and innocent curiosity with Wayne. When he seeks to re-connect with Wayne, he is denied twice, the first time when he attempts to connect with his supposed half-brother Bruce Wayne, the second time when he confronts Wayne himself at an opera. Wayne embarrasses him and slaps him in the face, infantilizing Arthur and accelerating the foreclosure of the father entirely.

In Lacan's theory of the mirror stage, the register of the imaginary is a conflictual psychic terrain in which the other grants the subject a sense of wholeness. The imaginary is formed in the mirror stage, typically when the child is between 6 and 18 months. In this period the identity of the child is formed in the mirror reflection it sees of its body. But this reflection is granted a sense of wholeness from the presence of a protective caretaker (mother or father typically). Thus, the other grants an imagined sense of wholeness to the subject that forms their ego. The film plays with mirrors frequently, and Joker often stares at his reflection in painful and empty reflection.

After Arthur experiences the embarrassment in his confrontation with Thomas Wayne, his situation deteriorates rapidly. His mother is hospitalized, he loses his job, and he loses government supported medical care and medication for his delusions and schizophrenia. With these losses, Arthur's delusions come apart, and he acts out by murdering three employees of Wayne Enterprises on the subway, an event that sparks insurrectionary sentiments in Gotham. Arthur, now properly identified by the public as Joker, becomes hailed as a hero even as his inner-psychic world begins to collapse. Arthur is not capable of working-through the profound aggressivity that has compounded over years of neglect. This culminates in a triggering event: he learns that Thomas Wayne was a figment of his mother's delusion, and he is not his father. Upon learning this Arthur lashes out and suffocates his mother.

Arthur's rage, combined with his mother's delusion of Wayne as his father, meant that by killing his mother, Arthur was also killing Wayne (the father of the imaginary). Wayne was the father of the imaginary riddled with an aggressivity that was overcome in the act of killing the mother as a fragment of the imaginary. But importantly, Wayne is not only the imaginary father, but also what Lacan calls a father of the Real, not only for Arthur but also for Gotham's proletarian underclass. Wayne is the

Power-Father that Freud discusses in *Totem and Taboo*; the father that the horde must get rid of for any possible justice to come about. At the crescendo of the film, Thomas Wayne is murdered by the mob, an act which for Freud symbolizes the opening of justice and of the equal distribution of enjoyment in society.

The murder of the primal father is the birth of the political. After these two murders, the beloved late-night TV host Murray Franklin invites Arthur to perform on his television show to poke fun at his odd and pathetic comedy bits. As we mentioned, Murray is effectively the father of the symbolic because he helped Arthur to mediate his fantasy of the social world, of recognition from institutions and so on. At this point in the film, Arthur is unmedicated, de-tethered from his mother's delusion, and he is channeling the insurrectionary energies that are elevating him to an antiheroic figure. He murders Murray in cold blood on TV, and like the murder of the mother/imaginary father, this act also entails a lucid break from Arthur's delusion. The Joker is born at this moment, and he importantly takes "society" as the responsible category for his situation. Proposing a satirical inversion of Thatcher's "there is no such thing as society"—Joker proclaims, "We live in a society!"

Joker abandons the superegoic function he had identified with Murray and transposes a new superego identification with the political uprising in Gotham and murders Murray in an act of new-found solidarity with his true origins—an anonymous (non-subject) orphan of the mob. Although he insisted in his exchange with Murray on the show that he is not "political", the Joker becomes a newly born political figure after ridding himself of the father of the imaginary and the symbolic. *Joker* plays out the very dark political situation of our present; the film is a portrayal of the collapse of the "social superego" and the reinvention of a new political mode founded on a destructive uprising of the mob. If the question of the "non-subject" at the foundation of political authority makes the question of the father a secondary question of identification, and indeed as Lacan points out, the father is a contingent function, then Joker stages the acceleration of capitalist de-territorialization in the context of a society in which the social superego has lost efficacy.

As Lacan points out in *Seminar I* (1953–1954), "the superego gives access to the root of the law itself, to that which is no longer of the order of language, but which nevertheless lies at the core of the commanding character of the law, in so far as nothing more than its root remains" (p. 102). *Joker* stages a dystopic re-composition of the superego, one which can be read as a reactionary portrayal of the Trump moment where Incels, social outcasts, lumpenproletariat, and so on can only find justice in a society that has abandoned them through fits of rage and orgiastic murder and mayhem. But it can also be read, as we have proposed here, as an insight into the birth of political contestations in a society that has completely abandoned large swaths of its citizenry.

The problem that non-subjects pose to the politics of the family are several: for starters, because they elude repression, authority, and representation, the non-subject reveals the function of the superego in its rawness. As we argued in this chapter, the non-subject opens the absence of the superego—as we saw in the case of Joker, the non-subject ushers in a completely new arrangement of the social order in which class struggle is named outright. The non-subject is typically deprived of family and initiation; they thus possess a certain wisdom of the "non-existent" social relation—the non-subject is thus plagued by the crisis of initiation differently than others who find more belonging in society. Despite all the inherent challenges to forging solidarities with non-subjects, any movement of liberation must forge strategies for incorporating non-subject positions.

REFERENCES

Badiou, A. (2012a). *The Rebirth of History*. Verso Books.

Badiou, A. (2012b). *The Rebirth of History* (G. Elliott, Trans.). Verso Books.

Clover, J. (2016). *Riot. Strike. Riot. The New Era of Uprisings*. Verso Books.

Davies, W. (2016, September–October). The New Neoliberalism. *New Left Review Issue*, 121–34.

Jameson, F. (1981). *The Political Unconscious*. Cornell University Press.

Lacan, J. (1947, January/March). British Psychiatry and the War January/March in L'duolution pychiatique, *Fascicule I.* 14–15.

Lacoue-Labarthe, P., & Nancy, J. (1997). *Retreating the Political,* S. Sparks (Ed.). Routledge.

Losurdo, D. (1996). Realism and Nominalism as Political Categories published in Presses Universitaires de France, Revue de Métaphysique et de Morale, Avril–Juin 1996, 101e Année, No. 2, Philosophie Politique (Avril–Juin 1996), pp. 211–223.

Moody, K. (2017). *On New Terrain: How Capital Is Reshaping the Battleground of Class War*. Haymarket Books.

Phillips, T. (Director) (2019) *Joker* [Film]. Warner Brothers.

Ronell, A. (2012). *Loser Sons: Politics and Authority*. University of Illinois Press.

Spillers, H. (1987). Mama's Baby, Papa's Maybe: An American Grammar Book. *Diacritics, 17*(2), Culture and Countermemory: The "American" Connection.

Stiegler, B. (2014). *The Lost Spirit of Capitalism: Disbelief and Discredit Malden*. Polity Press.

Tomšič, S. (2013). *The Capitalist Unconscious: Marx and Lacan*. Verso Books.

Tutt, D. (2021, March 4). Recentering the Lumpen Question Today: Understanding Lumpenization and Bonapartism. *Spectre Magazine*. See: https://spectrejournal.com/recentering-the-lumpen-question-today.

CHAPTER 10

Conclusion: Toward a Dialectics of Liberation

Abstract This chapter considers the superego dynamics on the contemporary left by looking at the interplay between what Mark Fisher called the Leninist superego and the cultural unconscious. The former tendency is militant, ascetic, and tends to be joy-less, whereas the latter is care-based, affective, and tends to conceive of revolutionizing everyday life, thus linking our time to the counterculture of the '60s and '70s. We discuss how these tendencies can introduce a politics of patience to forge greater solidarity and not see one another as antagonistic. We discuss the commune as an alternative form of the family, which may help subjectivity more adequately face the crisis of initiation and deal with Oedipal dynamics. We end with a discussion of the contemporary working-class family and the revolutionary potential of the black family as two family forms that are essential for any thinking or praxis of family liberation today.

Keywords Dialectics of liberation • Mark Fisher • Ellen Willis • Working-class family • The black family • Line of patience • Cultural unconscious

In conclusion, we aim to apply the concepts and problems we have tracked and identified thus far to some wider psycho-political dynamics within the politics of the family and liberationist politics more broadly. We have

© The Author(s), under exclusive license to Springer Nature Switzerland AG 2022
D. Tutt, *Psychoanalysis and the Politics of the Family: The Crisis of Initiation*, The Palgrave Lacan Series,
https://doi.org/10.1007/978-3-030-94070-6_10

argued that our time is marked by a superego that is far different than the form it took in Freud's time, and in this concluding chapter, we consider the political stakes of the 'social superego' from the perspective of liberation. The social superego does not elicit guilt in the subject; it more often produces shame, and shame is the affect that emerges when subjectivity is deprived of a social bond. When subjectivity is deprived of forming effective bonds, this also signifies a crisis of initiation.

The Freudian discovery and, later, Lacanian revision of Oedipus can be understood as a theory of subjective initiation. However, 'initiation' as a term should be understood as referring to what is being initiated is also that which is leaving. In the case of a theory of Oedipus as psychic liberation, the initiation at stake and involved with Oedipal subjectivization is that it signifies a movement out of the time of the father, a movement away from the family as a more oppressive and restrictive construct. Thus, the second aim of this conclusion is to think about how the family can be thought as a form that is more capable of nurturing subjective life in ways that promote joy, belonging, and growth, that is, a space where movement and initiation furthers subjective freedom for its members.

The superego is a regulator of psychic life, and it emerges in political moments of crisis, social antagonism, and uprising, which means that in our time, there are competing, more localized collective superego formations that contest the social superego. The consequence of this insight is that superego dynamics must be thought as alternative or competing forms from the predominant social superego. We already explored the historical tendencies of the liberal Oedipal problem and the insights we derived from these tendencies, which are embedded in Rawls and Emerson, is that there is also a liberal political superego.

To pick up from our argument in the chapter "Liberalism and the Oedipal," it is important to remember that liberalism tends to keep the paternal in an untranscendable position; therefore, liberal superegoic tendencies tend to latch onto actual authority figures more passionately in strong and seemingly ambivalent ways. The liberalist superego is thus not the best figure for thinking a more emancipatory break with the social superego because it often remains caught within a dynamic of submission to existing status quo power. In fact, when the liberal superego is triggered in situations of political struggle, it's often publicly and visibly opposed to more emancipatory political actors.

Why do we aim to think through what the prospect of a break with the social superego would entail? This draws us back into the wider background dynamic of late capitalism itself and the crisis of initiation it produces. Without addressing the root of the law as Lacan says of the superego, there is no chance to re-situate libidinal relations and, by extension, to restore greater freedom for subjectivity. The crisis of initiation is a more all-enveloping effect of late capitalist life, a general subjective crisis that envelops all subject positions.[1] It calls for a deeper consideration of the subject; it calls for making an inventory and an analysis of key figures of collective subjectivity. Our work in these last two chapters intends to open a few ideas toward this wider goal of thinking new ways of belonging, enjoyment, and the family form.

Just as we thought different subjective figures of politics in the previous chapter, and specifically, the figure of the "non-subject" was identified as an important figure for any thinking of political revolution and class struggle, we now turn to consider two predominant superegoic tendencies within liberation movements on the left—what we name the "cultural unconscious" and the "Leninist superego." We do not claim these two superegoic forms are the only two forms, but that they rather have historically experienced tension and often undermine one another in the wider work of organizing for liberation and emancipation. We are less interested in analyzing the liberalist superego, which also emerges as an often reactionary and detrimental force to the cause of liberation whenever it does emerge amid times of social and political conflict.[2]

One important insight the paradox of liberation has afforded us to locate is that liberationist proposals tend to destroy society's ego ideals and re-build a superego in the process. In this act of revolt and negation a series of superegoic tendencies also emerge concurrent to these political movements. Sometimes political movements such as the liberationist movements of the counterculture in the '60s and '70s can fall sway to this dynamic, and the downside becomes that the very force of antagonism

---

[1] We have chosen to focus on the working class, non-subjects such as the lumpenproletariat and later we will consider the black family. We have done this because we aim for a thinking of political liberation and how psychoanalysis can be furthered toward these ends. We maintain that middle classes and bourgeois classes are more often impediments to liberation than they are active agents in such efforts.

[2] The distinction we pinpoint here between the Leninist Superego and the cultural unconscious is not to be thought along the distinctions of subject positions—militant, obscure, reactionary, resurrection—as Badiou develops in *Logics of Worlds* (2006). This distinction is an internal distinction to the militant and faithful subject, to use Badiou's terminology. This is a problem within any thinking of the militant subject.

they pose to the status quo can diminish. It is true that counterculture demands dramatically diminished when they adopted a complicity with neoliberal entrepreneurial forms of freedom and abandoned the patient work of the revolution of everyday life. The paradox of liberation is at play here; it shows how the very radical demands remained in rhetorical and cultural form in public discourse, while the deeper political organizing that animated them largely dissipated.

The American cultural critic and socialist-feminist Ellen Willis refers to the legacy of the '60s and '70s counterculture as giving rise to a distinct "cultural unconscious." The cultural unconscious has been a site of contestation over the family and over the very politics of everyday life. For Willis (2014), the cultural unconscious is the main terrain of politics

> The imprint of what I call the cultural unconscious is stamped all over the present agonies of the American people: a citizenry buffeted by events, seemingly incapable of taking decisive collective action on serious social problems, passive in the face of an economy being transformed before our eyes, ambivalent to the point of schizophrenia on cultural issues. (p. 485)

Willis was a radical feminist cultural critic, theorist, and music writer for the Village Voice. She got divorced after a three-year marriage in her early 20s and dedicated her life to living on and off communes. Her writings on the Freudian left, the family and cultural politics are a significant contribution to the problematic of the paradox of liberation because she argues the liberatory promises of the '60s and '70s counterculture were rooted in impulses that revolved against the normalized and patriarchal expectations on marriage, sexuality, and the family.

Whether or not these movements were politically successful is a question of patience for Willis; that is, the labor of love involved in the revolution of everyday life is ongoing; there are no quick fixes to re-thinking relations of love and care, and in demanding greater leisure time from wage labor. Willis is not a "pro-family" advocate, and much of her work is a strong defense of twentieth-century socialist-feminists who put forward robust critiques of the patriarchal basis of power and hierarchy that the family engenders in society. She argues the true figure of a postpatriarchal family is the commune: a communally organized space where groups of people pool their resources and share housework and childcare. If such a commune structure were large enough it would effectively erase what Willis calls the "martyrdom structure" that is intrinsic to parenting and it would offer parents a release from the tension that comes with the fact that parenting is a 24-hour caretaking operation. Willis (2014) takes aim at what we have called the paradox of liberation, noting how '60s and '70s radicals failed to exert the proper patience to see the revolution of everyday life through and gave in to liberal entrepreneurial forms of self-liberation instead.

> The mentality that currently inspires sixties veterans to say things like "We didn't succeed in abolishing the family. This proves we were wrong—the family is necessary" is of a piece with the counterculture's notorious impatience. Our ambitions outstripped both the immediate practical possibilities and our own limitations. People turned themselves and each other inside out; terrible bitterness between women and men came to the surface; everything seemed to be coming apart, with no imminent prospect of our finding a better way to put it back together. A lot of people were relieved when the conservative mood of the seventies gave them an excuse to stop struggling and stretching themselves to uncertain purpose; a lot of men were particularly relieved when the backlash gave them support for digging in their heels against feminism. (p. 110)

Much has been written about the compromises of the '60s and '70s counterculture radicals, from different strands of feminists to family abolitionists and others.[3] But what Willis's diagnosis points out is the importance of bringing a patience to the work of revolution, a patience that is hard to muster because it must be brought into the otherwise mundane level of everyday life and culture. This is an area that the traditional left, especially elements of the far left, struggle to realize. In Mark Fisher's later work, specifically his *Acid Communism* (2018) writings, he was concerned with thinking through impediments to emancipatory movements and ways that collective joy and experimental art, aesthetics, and consciousness, that is, the revolution of everyday life—which includes a revolution of the family form—can be furthered.

What Willis and Fisher point to is less a paradox of liberation; this is after all a theoretical tool into the pitfalls and warnings implicit in liberation. What we are now talking about is a *dialectics of liberation* and how

---

[3] In this vein it is important to consider the new historical studies that have aimed to center the working class in the 60s and 70s cultural revolution in America. The films of Adam Curtis also paint a compelling perspective on the compromise and the paradox of liberation at the heart of those compromises. See Curtis, A. (2016) *Hypernormalization*.

the work of combining both the patience in thinking and in living more liberatory re-arrangements of everyday life can be combined with more large-scale contestations to the capitalist system itself. Fisher notes three figures of superego at play in the sort of dialectics of liberation we are speaking of:

> The first obstructive figure of the left was the complacent steward of Cold War organised labour or social democracy: backward-looking, bureaucratic, resigned to the "inevitability" of capitalism, more interested in preserving the income and status of white men than in expanding the struggle to include..., this figure is defined by compromise and eventual failure. The other figure—what I want to call the Harsh Leninist Superego—is defined by its absolute refusal of compromise. According to Freud, the superego is characterised by the quantitatively and qualitatively excessive nature of its demands: whatever we do, it's never enough. The Harsh Leninist Superego mandates a militant ascesis. The militant will be single-mindedly dedicated to the revolutionary event, and unflinchingly committed to the means necessary to bring it about. The Harsh Leninist Superego is as indifferent to suffering as it is hostile to pleasure Lenin's phobic response to music is instructive here: "I can't listen to music too often. It affects your nerves, makes you want to say stupid nice things and stroke the heads of people who could create such beauty while living in this vile hell. (Fisher 2018)

What Fisher pinpoints here is a problem of solidarity on the left that is concentrated within two predominant collective movements within the left: the Leninist superego and the cultural revolutionary.[4] The Leninist superego does not refer only to explicitly Leninist political activity, it also refers to a more general organizing tendency, a culture and ethos toward militant work which can encompass more traditional forms of socialism, Marxist-Leninist organizing, and social democracy. These are tendencies of group organization and of superegoic management that often work in opposition to one another. Any future left organizational success will be premised on the mastering of this chasm and in the capacity to exert the sort of patience that previous generations failed to bring about.

---

[4] Fisher is too dismissive of the "Leninist Superego." It has a history that stretches back to the Soviet period in which a multitude of pro-feminist, creative, and joyful expressions were also a part of militant political life. For example, there are several Bolshevik feminist authors to consider in this vein. The work of Boris Groys on Bakhtin's theory of the carnival, in "Between Stalin and Dionysus: Bakhtin's Theory of the Carnival" points to a possible direction in which a more joyful, less ascetic Leninist Superego might take.

Perhaps the task is to think a *line of patience* in conjunction with a *line of flight*. Such a politics of patience furthers the question of forging solidarity with the non-subject, this work involves the enhancement of care networks for whom inclusion is open to the subject positions that have been excluded by the neoliberal punitive order. This is not the place for a careful breakdown of the strategy of this patient politics, but an invitation to remain attentive to the political and the cultural unconscious. The cynicism of our age, in all its punitive discipline, surveillance and constant labor has resulted in a pessimism in the patient work of the revolution of everyday life. It has also made it more difficult to find the time necessary for the engaging in the equally patient work of political organization—labor organizing, protest, party formation, and so on. Both tendencies demand a politics of patience, especially given all the profound setbacks and defeats the left has faced in the post-2008 era. A joyful coexistence of revolutionary subjectivity must exist alongside a more ascetic and militant superego.

Fisher is right that the Leninist superego tends to treat the political dynamics of everyday life under capitalism with an answer of deferral: the question of how-to re-structure the way we live, make love, interact, and care for our children and so on will all come after the revolution. For that matter there are real debates in these two tendencies regarding how to create revolution. For example, the Leninist approach tends to emphasize revolution at the mode of production and works toward a worker-centered mode of praxis. The cultural unconscious aims to transform the sphere of culture and everyday life. Thus, what the cultural unconscious insists on furthering the proposal that that this work is already necessary; that is, the slow work of thinking and enacting different modes of living must happen continuously, even in moments where the political is seemingly absent. This was the animating force behind Fisher's *Acid Communism* project, a project that aims to infuse art and culture with a new sense of vibrancy and joy, against the often stultifying and depressive conditions of neoliberal everyday life.

To draw these insights back into the politics of the family, we must consider how the patient commitment to the revolution of everyday life, which the counterculture introduced, must also be thought as a commitment to thinking and experimenting with new forms of the family. The commune is one such proposal and despite many of the challenges this form presents in the era of punitive neoliberalism, the commune is an important alternative family form to think through. Although experiments in collective living tend to be short-lived and tend to emphasize lifestyle politics, to the extent that they even advocate politics at all, the commune form remains an important utopian form of thinking the family. It is important to think through the commune because it helps to bridge the prior dynamic, we identified, namely how do we continue in a more emancipatory political direction to fulfill the unmet promises of the '60s and '70s counterculture and its demands for a revolution of everyday life?

The family form that is discoverable in the commune helps to introduce a new imaginary of what a family structure might entail, including its division of labor, exchange of care and other techniques of family organization. The commune-form is one possible solution to the crisis of initiation and to the persistence of the social superego in the sense that if it is organized with explicit political ends for the revolution of everyday life, it maintains a potential for enacting and bringing about new forms of family organization that might better address Oedipalization.

Further study should be done to examine the basis by which Oedipal dynamics relate to and might function within the commune-form and changes in the structure of the family form would have to remain open to alteration accordingly. For example, what is the role of the father in a family organized as a commune? In Lacan's insight into the Names-of-the-Father we are led to assume that the commune form could more easily facilitate the movement out of the 'time of the father' and initiate new enjoyment for the subject because the father is multiple, contingent, and often random. If any experimentation in commune-form of the family is to be successful, it will maintain this element of openness and chance for subjectivity, which is an insight psychoanalysis offers to the family.

While the utopian idea of the commune-form of the family is important to enact, to experiment with and to further, we are also saddled with the reality that for most working-class people today the idea of finding the leisure time necessary to explore a mode of living on a commune is simply an impossibility. Punitive neoliberalism has re-shaped and intensified the hyper-marketization of the family, and in so doing it has made the family far less transcendable, both libidinally in terms of the crisis of initiation we have discussed, as well as materially. The conditions of discipline, indebtedness and precarity have entrenched more intensified inequality, a trend that mobilizes the family as a vector of wealth hoarding and inheritance. One of the biggest challenges to a socialist politics in our time is the fact that marriage now, more so than any time in recent memory, is mostly "assortative"; that is, people tend to find marriage partners from a similar class background. This is an outcome of the policies of the neoliberal era and the class dynamics that underpin them. These conditions make for a quasi-feudal form of love and mating; even though we do not live in a traditional arranged marriage culture, we now self-select marriage partners based on economic survival and these dynamics dominate even over love and the chance of romance.

This is a related example to the crisis of initiation in the sense that this trend indicates a profound rigidity of class alliance; that is, when people only marry those with similar incomes and educational backgrounds (Reeves and Venator, 2014), it creates wider social dynamics that affect the very possibility of forging solidarity across classes. More and more it seems that ideological fetishes emerge in the public discourse, from the anti-elite discourse on the right, to the veiled hatred of the uneducated working class on the liberal left, and these fetishes only conceal the deeper class chasm that truly animates and accounts for most political antagonisms in society. From a Marxist perspective, it is not only the proletariat that self-liberates itself; revolutions since the French Revolution up to May 1968 have depended on the building of solidarities across classes.[5]

In the prior chapter we argued that the subject position of those deprived of initiation, or non-subjects—what in Marxism is often referred to as the lumpenproletariat—are essential in thinking the reemergence of the political. But it is also important that we consider the composition of the working-class family in the era of punitive neoliberalism. How is the working-class family responding to the dynamics of the social superego in this era of punitive neoliberalism, and what about the ideological construct of the "family spirit" of the working class?

We argued in Chap. 2 that the working-class family has posed a contradiction to socialist-feminist proposals for the abolition of the bourgeois family stretching back to the very invention of the bourgeois family. The working-class family experiences the promise of the bourgeois family only in partial form. But what they are given of the family is still vital and catalytic to discovering the singularity of working-class subjectivity and value. The family thus becomes a place of utopian dreaming and longing. To

---

[5] It is an interesting fact that there was very little effective cross-class solidarity in the American Revolution, which even in Daniel Shay's Rebellion, the most militant of the revolutionary actions, was incapable of truly forging a bourgeois-proletariat solidarity. This is far different than the situation Europe faced in its revolutions, especially in the French Revolution for which many of the Jacobin leaders were all mostly from bourgeois classes themselves.

quote Lorraine Hansberry (2004) from the play "Raisin in the Sun," "[it] seem like God didn't see fit to give the black man nothing but dreams—but He did give us children to make them dreams seem worthwhile" (Act III).

To get at these questions of the contemporary working-class family, we once again turn to popular culture, by looking at how the dynamics of the working-class family are portrayed in the reboot of the popular TV show *Roseanne* in 2018. We then discuss the black working-class family, or the "black family" in America and its relation to the politics of the family. The experiences of the black family inform a great deal of insights for thinking and forging alternatives to the bourgeois family form.

In the *Roseanne* reboot, the Conner family is now all grown up, but the daughters Darlene and Becky are both living in extremely precarious situations: Darlene still lives at home in her 30s and Becky is planning to be a surrogate for another family to make extra money after her marriage ended in divorce. The *Roseanne* reboot presents all the post-2008 punitive dynamics placed on the family: the older daughter Darlene in her 30s and still living at home, can't find stable work, can't find a stable partner, and must sell her eggs for some extra spending money. The father Dan Conner has also lost stable work and has been forced into the gig economy. The family has no way to externally assign a cause to all this other than by the Algerist "individual choice" logic of American ideology. To the extent the family suffers, this suffering is reducible to family and individual idiosyncrasy. All the family has is themselves, and their humor becomes a means for survival.

Since all the precarious labor prospects fall back on the family to manage, the family has no means or way to understand the class dynamics that have captured them in this situation. The only line of flight from this condition is the cultivation of a humor of the absurd, which gets Roseanne in all sorts of trouble, both on-screen and off. The *Roseanne* reboot shows how the "family spirit" in the punitive neoliberal era enforces an even more precarious and more desperate family spirit for the working class. Its mantra seems to be: "all we have is the family," even though the family is the site of a great repression in the sense that its suffering, brought on by class disadvantage and precarity, are not spoken of. To the extent the family's suffering is addressed at all, it is through humor and the more ordinary forms of intimate support and care.

The magnitude of difficulties that befall the contemporary working-class family are immense and the political alternatives to escaping these conditions, at least as currently available, have not produced any viable path of structural change. Dan Conner (the father) attempts to re-introduce a sort of "hard hat Nixonian" brand of politics, but it feels immediately nostalgic and ineffectual with the realities of the gig economy and the absence of organized labor protections. Roseanne opines at times for the loss of traditional parenting and attempts to blame her children's reliance on the family on society's loss of traditional family values. But even this suggestion is cynically adopted, and no one quite seems to believe it. Ideologically, nothing works. All positions that offer solutions to the predicament seem to fall apart and don't amount to anything. All that is left over in the show is humor and cynical moralism and the two seem to intersect repeatedly. The fact that all these precarious dynamics led to Roseanne Barr (in real life) getting cancelled and written out of the show for racism only goes to show the profound *nominalism at the heart of contemporary politics* and the profound interlinkage of class and race antagonisms that they produce.

Although the era of punitive neoliberalism exerts these pressures on the family, it is essential to understand these pressures have long afflicted the black family in America. For Hortense Spillers, the black family is like a "captive body" that typical gender distinctions and divisions of labor that occur within the bourgeois family, are totally collapsed within the black family. Spillers (1987) argues that for the black family the very value the family is meant to produce. The black family moves outside of the "dominant symbolic order." In our analysis of the crisis of initiation, this means that the black family is an example of a family structure that has effectively survived based on another sort of initiation than the bourgeois family. As a result of a long history of family violence brought on by conditions of racial oppression, categories such as "kin," and "gender formation" have no decisive legal or social efficacy for the black family (pp. 67–68).

Spillers echoes an insight of the socialist-feminist theorist Angela Davis, who notes that black people's efforts to hold on to and strengthen their family ties were cruelly assaulted, for generations. Yet in the face of this assault on the black family, the structure of the family has remained an important cauldron of resistance, forging and preserving a vital legacy of collective struggle for freedom. The brutal economic and political pressures connected with slavery and continuing throughout subsequent historical eras have inevitably prevented the black family patterns from conforming to the dominant family models. In any conversation of what a more revolutionary model of the family might look like, what shape it might take, we have a historical experience in the black family that is essential to tap into, to learn from.

As Davis and Spillers both argue in different ways, the black family possesses a strength through resistance to state violence and racial exclusion. The black family has had to creatively build a family based on survival and to link this to our concept of initiation; we can say the black family is an example of counter-initiation, of forging a solidarity and familial network that forms beyond the bourgeois family spirit. It is not surprising that in the early period of neoliberalism during the Reagan presidency the black family was the first familial unit to be penalized and blamed for the rise of social ills such as teenage pregnancy, gun violence, and crime.[6]

This analysis leaves us with a series of questions: how does the black family relate to the liberal Oedipal problem? One possibility is that the paternalistic basis of liberal politics elicits a certain attractiveness for the black family given its long history of exclusion from the bourgeois family form. This can be witnessed in the turn to a more conservative and traditionalist turn within contemporary black politics. On the other hand, the black family is a truly elastic and resilient family form, and this resilience is not of the same form as the resilience of hyper-marketization precisely because for so long the black family has been forced to derive value outside of inclusion in the market. It is this well of insight that can inform more experimental arrangements of the family.

What we have aimed to put forward in these last two chapters is the importance of identifying and giving shape to subjective figures of the politics of the family and to think both how intensifying class dynamics are affecting the family and how to forge solidarities to confront these challenges across class. It is not an empty cliché to say that overcoming the dynamics of our present social and political order requires building solidarities across class and racial divides. This remains of utmost importance in any re-thinking of the family form. We have proposed more thinking on the commune as a site where experimentation in the family can be furthered and that such experiments may suggest fruitful connections to other projects of emancipatory politics.

---

[6] For more on the policing of the black family through social policy, see Cooper M.'s discussion of the Moynihan Report on *Family Values*, and Angela Davis and Fania Davis, The Black Scholar, September/October 1986, Vol. 17, No. 5, THE BLACK FAMILY: 1986 (September/October 1986), pp. 33–40.

A method of advocating greater social protections and welfare state support to the family is another avenue of enacting the necessary relief that working-class families need today. However, the post-Occupy left attempts to enact these reforms in the movements of Bernie Sanders and Jeremy Corbyn have not succeeded but have been overwhelmed by a retrenched liberal tidal wave. The task of the left must involve a careful attention to the libidinal dynamics that impede solidarity, and this text has aimed to offer insight into these forces of anti-solidarity and have hinted at some directions for overcoming them.

In his later work Deleuze (2002) once wrote, of the family:

We should get to the point of being able to say: your father, your mother, your grandmother, everything is fine, even the Name of the father, every entry is fine from the moment there are multiple exits (p. 76).

REFERENCES

Badiou, A. (2006). *Logics of Worlds* (Alberto Toscano, Trans.). Continuum Press.

Boris, G. (2017). Between Stalin and Dionysus: Bakhtin's theory of the carnival. *Dialogic Pedagogy: An International Online Journal, 5.* https://doi.org/10.5195/dpj.2017.212. http://dpj.pitt.edu

Curtis, A. (2016). Hypernormalization. *BBC News.* See https://youtu.be/AUiqaFIONPQ

Deleuze, G. (2002). *Dialogues II: Gilles Deleuze and Claire Parnet* (E. Albert, Trans.). Continuum.

Fisher, M. (2018). *Acid Communism* (Unfinished Introduction). See Blackout Poetry and Politics. https://my-blackout.com/2019/04/25/mark-fisher-acid-communism-unfinished-introduction/

Davis, A., & Davis, F. (1986, September/October). *The Black Family.* The Black Scholar 1986, *17*(5), 33–40.

Hansberry, L. (2004). Mama to Ruth. Act III. *A Raisin in the Sun.* With an Introduction by Nemiroff, R. Vintage.

Reeves, R. V., & Venator, J. (2014, February 10). *Opposites Don't Attract: Assortative Mating and Social Mobility.* https://www.brookings.edu/blog/social-mobility-memos/2014/02/10/opposites-dont-attract-assortative-mating-and-social-mobility/

Groys, B. (2017). Between Stalin and Dionysus: Bakhtin's Theory of the Carnival. *Dialogic Pedagogy: An International Online Journal, 5.* https://doi.org/10.5195/dpj.2017.212. http://dpj.pitt.edu

Spillers, H. (1987). Mama's Baby, Papa's Maybe: An American Grammar Book. *Diacritics, 17*(2), Culture and Countermemory: The "American" Connection (Summer, 1987), 64–81.

Williams, M. (2018). *Roseanne* ABC Network.

Willis, E. (1979, September). *The Essential Willis* "The Family: Love It or Leave It." *Village Voice.*

Willis, E. (2014). *The Essential Ellen Willis,* Nona Willis Aronowitz (Ed.). University of Minnesota Press.

Glossary of Key Concepts

Counter-initiation A more contingent subjective process in which the subject undergoes initiation without the support or aid of a traditional family. A contingent type of initiation in which subjects invent strategies for surviving and resisting a world that has mostly abandoned them.

Cultural Unconscious A concept coined by Ellen Willis that refers to the affective, sexual, and libidinal investments at stake in political discourse. The cultural unconscious is the site where the libidinal stakes of the culture war and debates over the family, abortion, tradition, and so on are won or lost.

Dialectics of Liberation An antonym to the paradox of liberation, dialectics of liberation is a theory meant to work through antagonistic superegoic tendencies that often compete in any given liberatory or emancipatory political movement.

Family Spirit A logic and ideology that enables a family to maintain the illusion of its identity as a separate entity from the sphere of social reproduction and labor. The family spirit is an invention of the bourgeois family, and it is derived through the forms of symbolic exchange that occur within the family.

Hyper-marketization of Everyday Life The capitalist process following the '60s and '70s counterculture demands for a "revolution of everyday life." Hyper-marketization of everyday life is the tendency within the

D. Tutt, *Psychoanalysis and the Politics of the Family: The Crisis of Initiation*, The Palgrave Lacan Series, https://doi.org/10.1007/978-3-030-94070-6

neoliberal order for every sphere of life to become overwhelmed with market and utilitarian logics, and the tendency also for the marketization to absorb the rhetoric of liberation.

Initiation A subjective process that can involve rituals, rites, and unconscious forms of working-through identifications, attachments, and affects. Initiation generally refers to any event, subjective process, rite, or ritual that enhances the subject's capacities to flourish or gain a degree of subjective freedom and responsibility.

Liberal Oedipal Problem The tendency of liberal theories of the subject and liberal principles of equality and justice to rely on a paternalistic mode of authority that places authority figures in a paternalistic and untranscendable position.

Line of Patience A play on Deleuze and Guattari's "line of flight," referring to the patience at stake in working through political liberation and not succumbing to the marketization of the demands of a given political liberation movement.

Non-subject Subject positions deprived of initiation and who tend to be barred from inclusion in productive labor and social reproduction. Non-subjects are typically associated with the *lumpenproletariat* or the nomadic proletariat in Marxist thought.

Oedipus A subjective process of working through paternal identifications within institutional and familial contexts. A theory for the invention of a new desire, signifying movement, not stasis.

Paradox of Liberation A dynamic facing liberatory movements when they must confront the collapse of the ego ideals and superego they revolted against and the concurrent challenge implicit in managing their own superego formation.

Social Superego The predominant tendency of the superego in late capitalism. It refers to the ways superego enforcement derives more from the market's logic and force than from groups, collectives, and families.

Index[1]

[1] Note: Page numbers followed by 'n' refer to notes.

CPSIA information can be obtained
at www.ICGtesting.com
Printed in the USA
LVHW081204080522
718198LV00006B/348

9 783030 940690